Talks
About Art

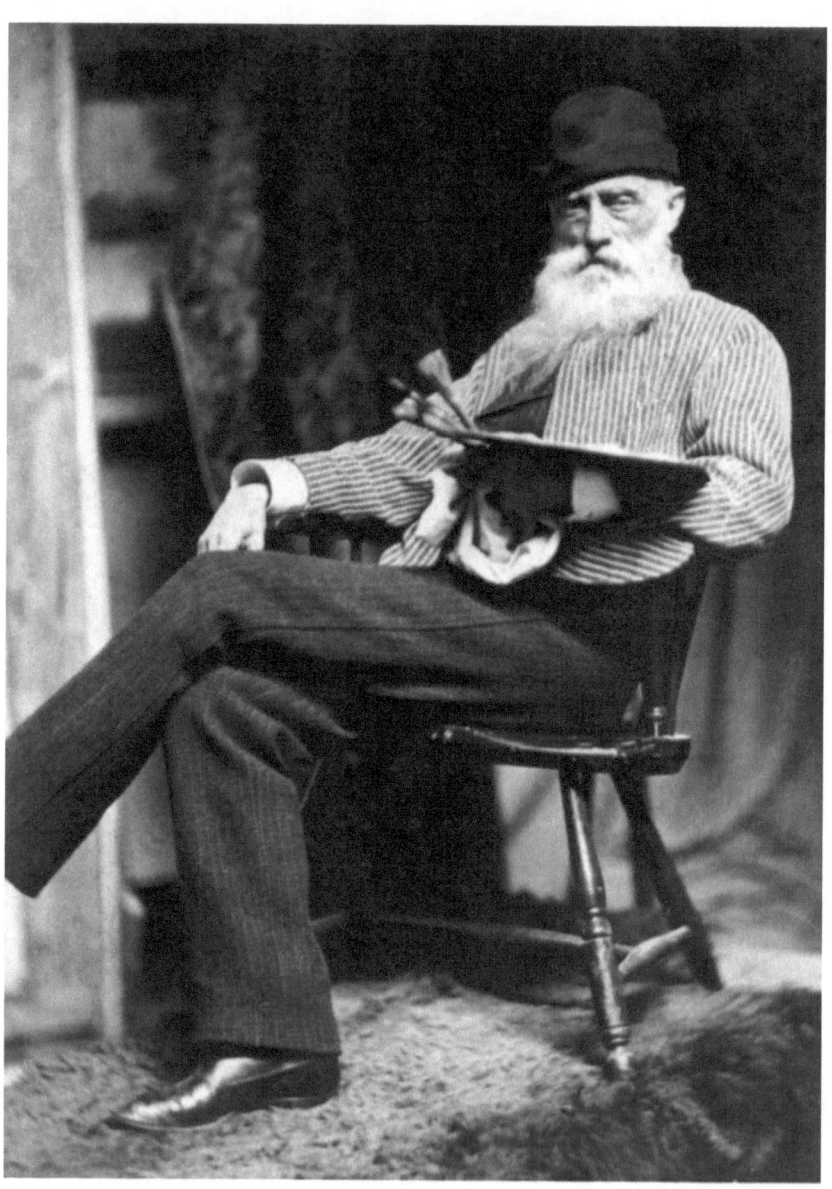

Talks
About Art

WILLIAM MORRIS HUNT

extracts of advice to his students
compiled in 1877 by

Helen M. Knowlton

with a biography by

Edward Waldo Emerson

originally published in 1915 in
"The Early Years of the Saturday Club, 1855-1870"

contributions by
Lowes Dickinson
Sir John Everett Millais R.A.
Robert Browning
William Blake
William Hazlitt
John Ruskin

PERUSE PRESS
LOS ANGELES

Title:
Talks About Art

Author:
William Morris Hunt

Contributors:
Edward Waldo Emerson
Helen M. Knowlton
Sir John Everett Millais R.A.
Lowes Dickinson
Robert Browning
William Blake
William Hazlitt
John Ruskin

Editor:
Mark Diederichsen

Publisher:
Peruse Press
Los Angeles, California

First Peruse Press edition

First printing 2013

Front cover:
William Morris Hunt
The Gleaner
1865
oil on canvas
Museum of Fine Art, Boston

Back cover:
William Morris Hunt
Self Portrait
1866
oil on canvas
Metropolitan Museum of Art

Frontispiece:
James Wallace Black
William Morris Hunt
1879
silver print
Smithsonian Archives of American Art

ISBN-13: 978-0615882703
ISBN-10: 0615882706

CONTENTS

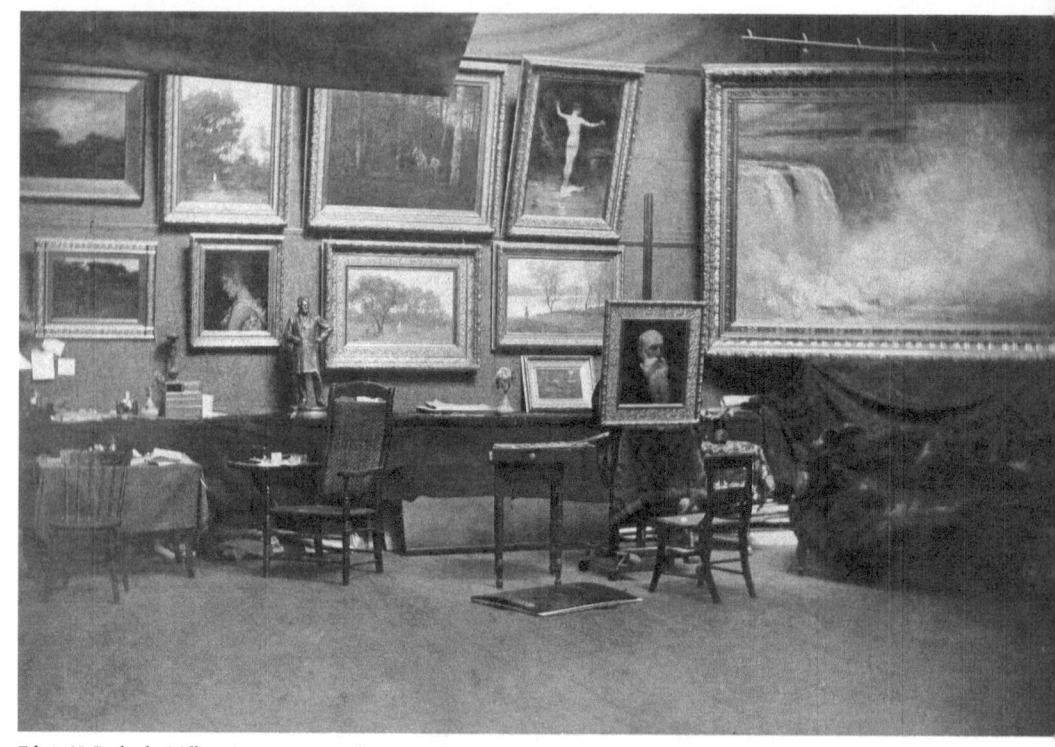

Edwin N. Peabody, *William Morris Hunt studio,* 1879, silver print, Smithsonian Archives of American Art.

WILLIAM MORRIS HUNT
1824-1879

WILLIAM MORRIS HUNT was born in Brattleboro, Vermont, and his father dying when his children were all very young, their mother, a superior woman, whose yearnings for art as a girl had been frowned on, determined to give her five children every opportunity. She moved to New Haven, found an Italian artist, and she and all of them took lessons of him. Richard, the second son, became a distinguished architect. William at sixteen entered Harvard, was a bright scholar, but the artistic temperament compelled him to music, drawing, and to the woods and meadows. So, as "too fond of amusement," he was rusticated to Stockbridge — no hardship for him. Some one there, perhaps the clergyman who had him in charge, saw in him "A soul let loose, an inspiration to all who met him."

Troubled by William's persistent cough, Mrs. Hunt determined that he should not return to college then, and with all her children valiantly sailed for Italy. This changed the course of William's life. It had been planned that, after a year, he should go back, finish his course at Harvard, and then study to be a surgeon. Rome decreed that he should be an artist; his passion for art led his mother to stay abroad with her family. He wished to be a sculptor, and began modelling in the studio of H. K. Brown.

Copying the work of the past in Rome did not appeal to William, but he found delight in Paris where he worked under

Barye, meaning to become a sculptor. Then, following the custom of the times, he went to Dusseldorf and began the usual drill there. He hated it and went away. On his return to Paris he saw

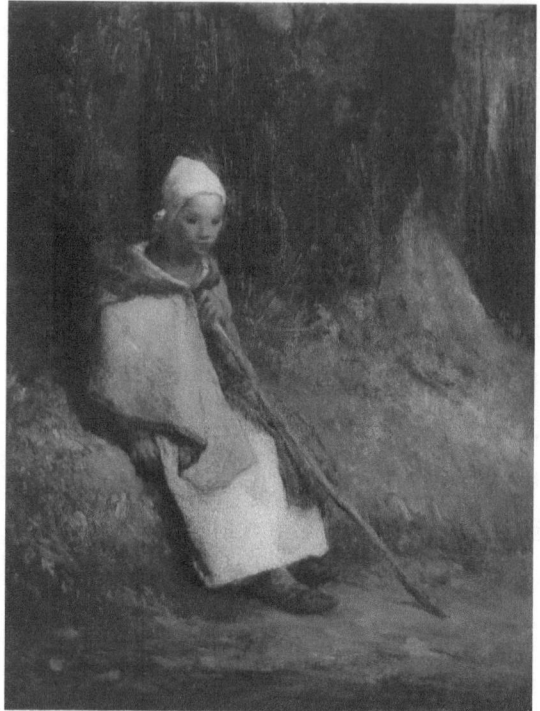

Shepherdess Sitting at the Edge of the Forest, c. 1848, oil, 12x9 inches, Museum of Fine Arts, Boston.

in a window the "Falconer," by Couture. Stirred by this, he entered Couture's studio. The master looked over his work from the life model before him and said, "But you do not know how to draw," and introduced him to values, the foundation of good work.[1] This, and the confirming his instinct that the artist must paint for joy, were what he learned from Couture. He soon found that he had all that this master could give him.

He then began studying the work of the great Venetians and Flemings, but one day saw Millet's "Sower," great, but unappreciated, in exhibition, and recognized a prophet and more than a prophet. The eager youth went to Barbizon. There he found this noble peasant painting in a cellar the life of the toiling human beings about him. On the easel was the "Sheep Shearers." Hunt reverenced him from

1. In his admirable *Méthode et Entretiens d'Atelier* Couture tells the story of his opening the eyes of a confident student of Dusseldorf academic training to values, in an interesting way. It was probably Hunt.

that moment. More than that, this joyous youth made Millet
his friend. He soon moved to Barbizon and was in close relation with him for two years, a disciple, not an imitator. Hunt
did great service to Millet who
more than repaid it by the lift
he gave to him by his high tone,
his breadth, his seriousness;
more than all, under his influence Hunt's boyish generosity
became human sympathy.
Hunt sold the "Sheep Shearers"
for Millet to Mr. Brimmer, and
when he gave him the money,
the great painter said he had
never before had a hundred
dollars in his hand. Thus, and
by all the purchases he could
afford, the young American
lifted the master out of debt

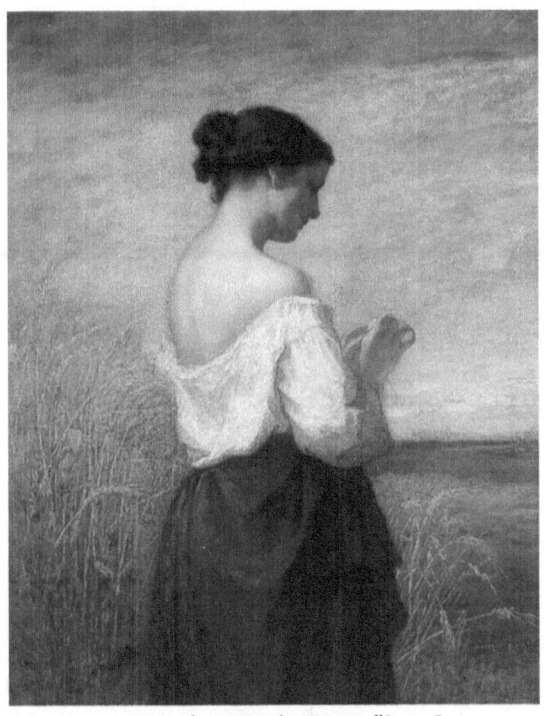

Paysanne, circa 1852, oil, 66x35 inches, Musee d'Orsay, Paris.

and, more than that, gave vogue to his pictures.

In the Fontainebleau region Hunt met the group of painters
then making fame for the "Barbizon School" against the tide.
It is said that Diaz told an American that Hunt was the most
brilliant man he had ever known. Hunt kept and rejoiced in
a beautiful pair of horses and drawn swiftly by them saw the
region around Paris. Full of youthful vitality, and enjoyment
of nature and of people, it was well that he found in Millet a

chastening influence. Millet took interest in his pictures, and, struck with his facility, said, "Hunt, you ought to work!" Yet he was by no means idle and many admirable works were done

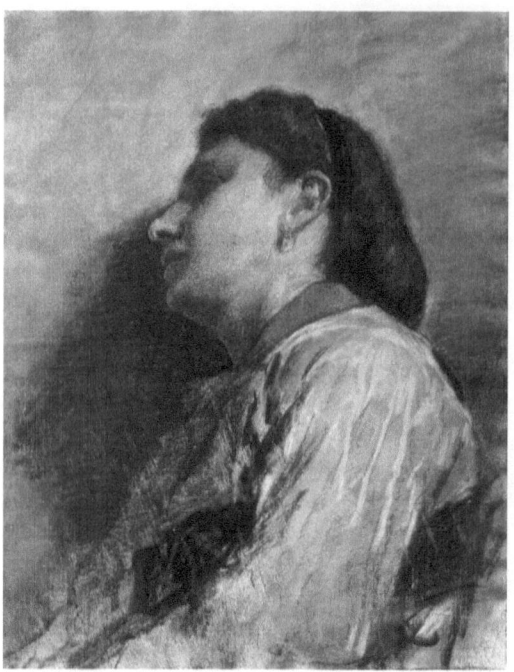

in France, like the "Prodigal Son," the queenly portrait of his mother, the "Fortune-Teller," the first "Marguerite." Napoleon III twice tried to buy the last-mentioned work in vain, as it was promised to an American. Long retaining his interest in sculpture, Hunt kept up relations with Barye, believing him and Millet the greatest artists of their time.

In 1855, Mr. Hunt, returning to this country, was married, and made his pleasant year-round

Head of a Lady, charcoal, 22x17 inches, Museum of Fine Arts, Boston.

house in Newport among agreeable neighbours, especially Henry James, Sr., and his young family. As a school-boy visiting in that wonderful home, I had the privilege of going to Hunt's studio where William and La Farge were the *élèves*. While I was there Hunt came In and cordially asked me, boy as I was, to his studio upstairs. There he showed me, to my great delight, the first studies for his wonderful "Anahita," or "Flight of Night," which years later adorned the Capitol at Albany. He also showed me the charming lithographs from his paintings, such as the "Hurdy-Gurdy Boy" and the "Girl at the Fountain." He gave me copies of these and more. Hunt, In his charming way, seemed to know no age in persons who were Interested in beautiful things. This was about 1859. That same year, at the request of the Essex Bar, he painted the remarkable portrait of Chief Justice Shaw, now in the Salem Court-House.

He soon established himself in Roxbury. Later, he had a studio in Summer Street where he introduced Bostonians to the canvases of Millet, Diaz, Rousseau, Géricault, and Corot, new to most of them; yet the artist's masculine enthusiasm and hospitable charm were the principal attraction.

His characteristic generosity appeared in his calling on the young men returning from study abroad, and he almost always bought a picture to help bring them into notice. Seeing some of the work of Vedder, a stranger to him, he wrote to urge him to exhibit in Boston, and many of the pictures were at once sold.

Stirred by an attack in the *Advertiser* from some authority at Harvard, on the modern French painters, Hunt replied in a withering article: "The standard of art education is indeed carried to a dizzy height in Harvard University when such men as Millet are ranked as triflers. . . . Which one of the painters named above was not more familiar with Veronese's best work than are our children with the Catechism? They were not only familiar with all that is *evident*, but devoted students of the qualities in Veronese, of which few besides themselves know. It is not worth while to be alarmed about the influence of French art. It would hardly be mortifying If a Millet or a Delacroix should be developed in Boston. It is not our fault that we Inherit Ignorance In art; but we are not obliged to advertise it."

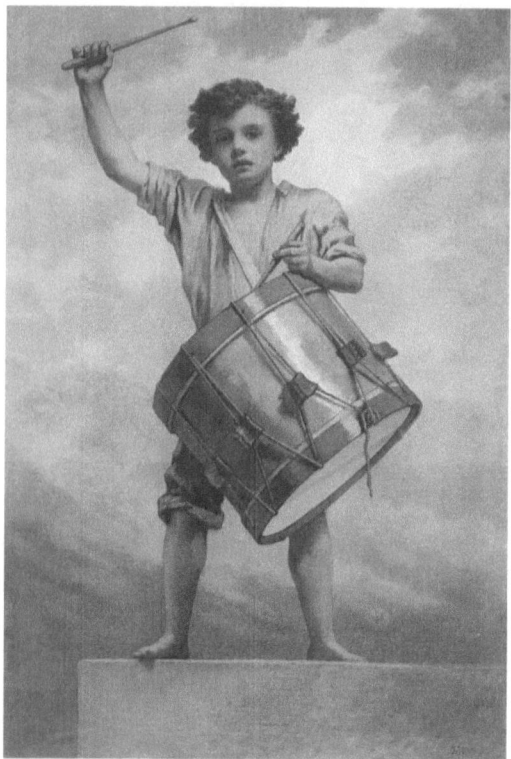

Drummer Boy, 1862-65, charcoal, Museum of Fine Arts, Boston.

The first year of the war brought out Hunt's Inspiring "Drummer Boy" beating "To Arms!" and the magnificent "Bugle Call." The power and beauty of his portraits began to be appreciated in Boston. Sometimes he was not successful because he required that the sitter should lend himself freely to the work. Thus, a portrait of Dr. Holmes was prosperously begun, but the Doctor unhappily took out his watch, having an engagement in Cambridge, and asked, "How long must I sit?" Hunt, somewhat disturbed, yet set to work, and all was going well when the watch and the uneasy expression reappeared. These conditions soon wrecked the adventure. Emerson disliked even to sit for a photograph; said he "was not a subject for art;" but Mrs. John M. Forbes wished much that Hunt should paint him! He was eager to do It, and began In good hope. But, though Emerson liked him, the sittings dismayed him, and when, on leaving, he asked, "Must I come again?" Hunt told him No, it was of no use. Hunt used to say, "No persuaded sitters for me: I never could paint

a cat if the cat had any scruples, religious, superstitious, or otherwise about sitting." Emerson's unfinished portrait perished in the Boston Fire. At the desire of a committee appointed to have a portrait of Sumner painted, as a gift to Carl Schurz, Hunt somewhat unwillingly consented to undertake it, for he found himself repelled by the Senator's personality. Probably he had only met him at the Club, where Sumner's magisterial bearing, lack of flexibility and of humour

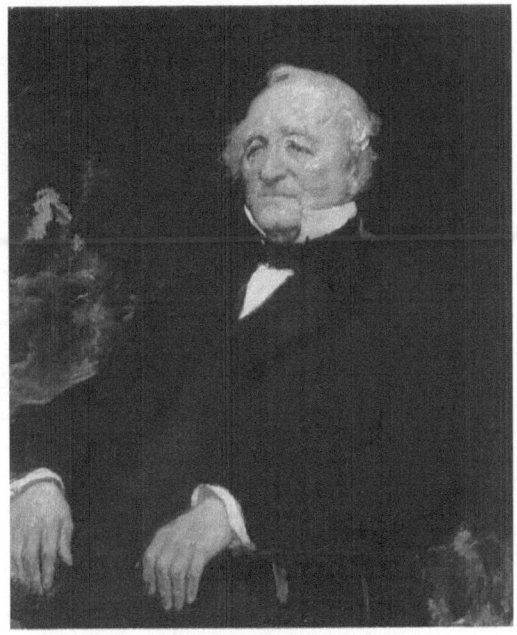

Senator Charles Sumner, circa 1870, oil, 36x29 inches, Museum of Fine Arts, Boston.

were sometimes annoying. The committee did not like the portrait. Hunt painted what he found in Sumner's face and bearing, his confident and almost scornfully militant side. The picture won much praise in England.

Hunt's brilliant yet human presence, his original force and great generosity leavened the inert lump of art opinion in Boston. He awakened the Interest and desire of the young people, and consented to take charge of a class of forty young women. His instruction to his pupils was original, exciting;

if necessary, wisely contradictory, to suit the individual temperament. More than all, he Inspired them with love of art and made it seem possible to them. He was not one of those Instructors who simply pass by the pupil and, when asked for a criticism, coldly say, "I see nothing *there* to criticise," utterly discouraging. Hunt could not but inspire by his wit and his faith. Fortunately one of his pupils, as he passed from easel to easel, jotted down his quick criticisms and remarks on the corner of her drawing-paper. Later, when Hunt became more busy, he deputed the business management of the class to this young lady. Mr. Lowes Dickinson, the English portrait painter. Impressed by Hunt's Chief Justice Shaw, visited the class. After Hunt had taken leave, this lady, Miss Helen Knowlton, showed him her notes of the master's varied Instruction. Mr. Dickinson was so struck with their value that he urged the printing of these *Talks on Art*, to which Hunt at last consented after pruning them severely.[2]

Hunt's disappointing lack of interest In the School of Drawing and Painting in the new Museum of Fine Arts was due to disbelief in the South Kensington ideas that at first prevailed. His own Dusseldorf experience, also the influence of Couture — who, like himself, had been paralyzed by academic work — made him dread the usual routine of school Instruction, endless crayon stump work from cast and model. He wished rather for the Museum School a great working *atelier* where many live painters should give each one day a

---

2. We owe also to Miss Helen Knowlton her admirable *Art Life of William Morris Hunt* from which the writer has gratefully quoted much.

week. Thus he hoped for freshness and individuality and the personal magnetism of one or another to stir the individual pupil. When asked what should be the limit of age for study In the Art Museum, he replied: "From the age when Beethoven began to play the piano — four years — to the age when Titian painted one of his greatest pictures — ninety years."

One of Hunt's sayings was, "Queer old thing painting is; but we would rather die doing it than live doing anything else." He defined painting as, "Having something to say, and not saying it in words."

Catholic In his receptivity, he recognized the quality In Japanese art. Mr. Norton sitting beside Hunt at a Club dinner, told him of a beautiful little Japanese vase or cup which he had just come by, and said, "Would you like to see it." taking it from his pocket and handing it to him. Hunt exclaimed, "Like to see it! By God, it's one of those damned ultimate things!"

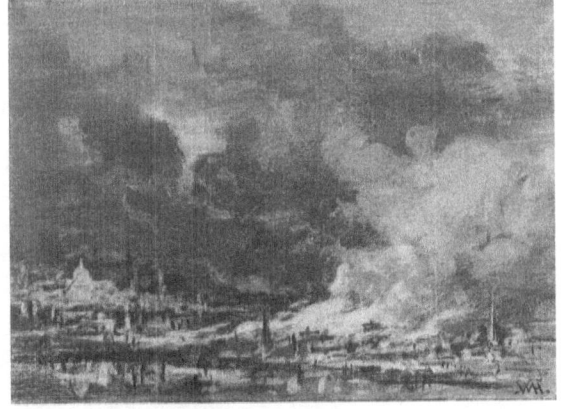

The Boston Fire, 1872, charcoal, 8x11 inches, Museum of Fine Arts, Boston.

The Great Fire in Boston in 1872 swept Summer Street and with it Hunt's studio and all its contents, many notable portraits in all stages of work, and also his own valuable collection of the paintings of the French masters whom he held in honour.

After this time Hunt turned more to landscape painting

than he had hitherto. As he advanced In It, his pleasure seems to speak from his canvas. Mr. Forbes valued Hunt highly and he took him with him as his guest, In 1874, to Florida, where he went for rest when overworked — rest, however, of an active-out-of-door kind; first for shooting and fishing along the coast,

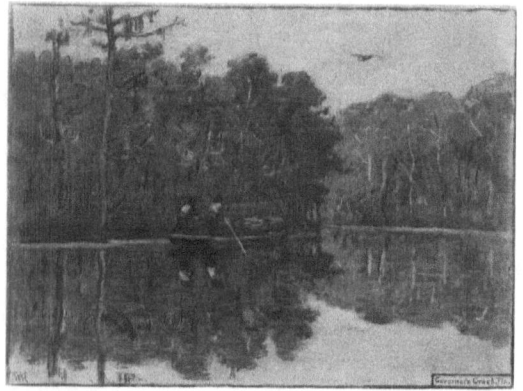

Governor's Creek, Florida, 1873, charcoal, 8x11 inches, Museum of Fine Arts, Boston.

then to his family cottage at Magnolia Springs. Here Hunt delighted in the wide gleaming St. John's River, seen through the steely glitter of the great magnoHas, and to sketch, on the strange lonely creeks, their live-oaks and cypresses hung by the half-mourning moss swaying slowly in the breeze.

In the years Immediately following he painted the upper Charles, then the Artichoke River at Curzon's Mills, with constantly increasing light and colour. In some of these pictures one sees the effect of the teacupful of opals which he bought in Mexico as a lift.

In the spring of 1878, Hunt went to Niagara for rest, but, stirred by the wild rush of the rapids, the wonderful colour and the majesty of the Falls, sent for paint and canvas and worked with great results. I cannot, while telling of the Niagara vacations, omit a story of Miss Knowlton's which shows Hunt's tenderness. Returning to their hotel, his sister told him that, while buying some bead-work in a small shop, she had been distressed by hearing a sick child cry in the back room. She was sure that it must be suffering greatly. Its screams still pierced her ears.

"I believe," said her brother, "that I can cure that child; and what is more, I am going to do it." He arose from his

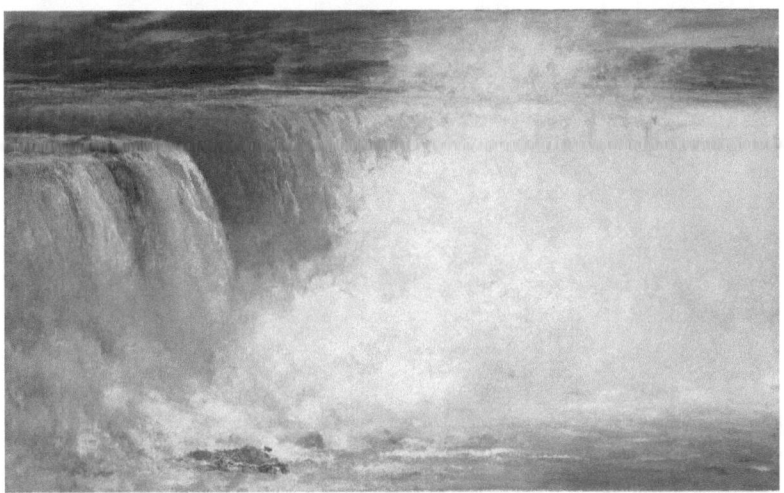

Niagra, 1879, oil, 62x99 inches, Museum of Fine Arts, Boston.

chair, called for his overshoes; it was half-past nine o'clock in the evening, dark and raining; but he would go. He learned where the shop was, and set forth hastily. At one o'clock in the morning he returned, wet, but very happy.

"How's your child?" his sister asked.

"She's all right. I left her sleeping. I tell you, that kind of work pays!"

But midsummer of that year brought to Hunt a call, unexpected, unhoped-for, to do a great public work, in the toil and the joy of which his life culminated. The work was noble and worthy; it stirred and inspired him — happily not foreseeing the sad end. He was commissioned to adorn with great mural paintings the Assembly Hall of the New Capitol at Albany.

On a scaffold forty feet above the floor. Hunt painted, directly on stone, the many colossal figures of his two symbolic designs, "The Discoverer" and "The Flight of Night." With but one assistant he did this great work in two months.

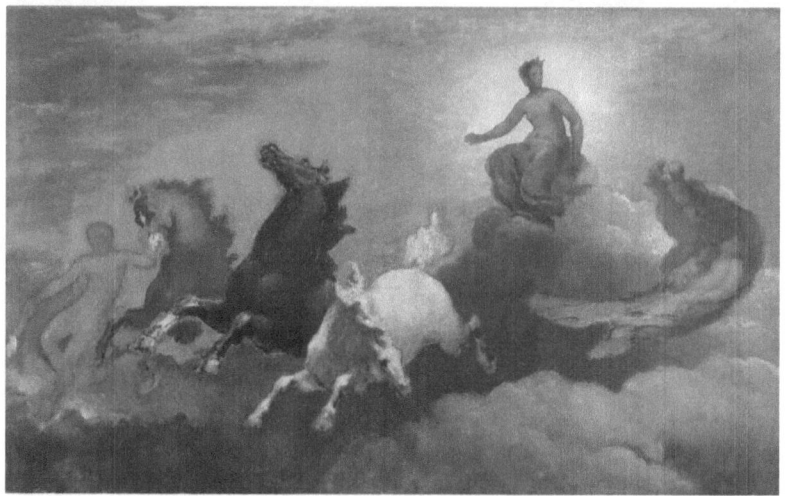

Anahita. The Flight of Night, 1878, oil, 62x99 inches, Museum of Fine Arts, Boston.

Hunt felt freedom and advance in this new work. "Think of it, you never hear of Boston a hundred miles away! I am out of the world, and I want to stay out." But with this enthusiasm in a great work went pleasure in, and reverence for, the workmen; he painting, they building, six hundred men together, each respecting and enjoying the other's work. They said that while they were proud to be working on such a building, they were prouder still to see his work going on. "I tell you," said Hunt, "that I never felt so big in my life as I did when they asked me if they could come again and see my picture." He planned, in other paintings there (vetoed later by the Governor), to introduce their figures.

Before beginning the work, Hunt had faithfully tried, as far as the time allowed, in the summer, the effects of moisture and of cold on paint on stone, and believed it would last. But unhappily politics had crept into the contracting, a leaking roof resulted, and within ten years the paintings were utterly ruined. But the artist was spared this blow. Inevitable reaction had followed the supreme mental and physical expenditure; personal sorrows were added. In the summer of 1879, weak and depressed, he sought refreshment with friends at Appledore Island. There, whether by accident or sudden impulse, he was drowned in an inland pool in the early autumn.

Mr. Hunt was a most striking personality, tall and spare, with brilliant eyes and an aquiline nose; nearly bald, but with a forelock like Time in the Primer, a moustache and long gray beard. He was quick and alert, most cheery and responsive; a wonderful *raconteur* and even mimic, everything became dramatic in his handling.

A lady, a guest with him at the enchanting Isle of Naushon, riding in a party with Mr. Forbes on the "Desert," describes Hunt's sudden appearance on a fine Kentucky horse, riding up gallantly, his beard blown backward on both shoulders, the sunset gleaming like garnet in his eyes, and the Mephisthophelean effect heightened by a turkey feather springing from each side of his soft hat. Yet in his studio in serious mood, with his round cap and velvet coat, he was singularly suggestive of Titian's portrait of himself. In Hunt's early days an elderly stranger in France came up and said, "Sir, you so much resemble a great Frenchman whom I knew that it seems as if he must have returned to earth." "That is indeed strange," was the reply; "to whom do you refer?" "To Géricault."

In sympathy and respect Hunt knew no social class. He honoured the labourer; helped, in the city street, on the instant, the poor woman with her ash-barrel, or, in a humble house, a stranger mother to relieve the pain of her sick child.

From Hunt's work beauty in its full sense speaks, contrasted with that of many men eminent for technique or "strength." In his is nothing coarse, sensational, ignoble, ugly. He heeded the words of his old master. Couture, *"Avant tout, fuyez le laid!"* In his work is always feeling and humanity. Mrs. Whitman, perhaps his best pupil, said, "Even what is called the moral passion has a place in his art."

After his death these maxims of Hunt were found in his pocket- book: "To be strong, get self-control; to be strong, live for others; no one ever injures us, we injure ourselves."

Once, when asked to write in a painter's album, this was his contribution :

"Go East, young man! Meeting, greet the sun, our master-painter . . . tell him that the light which he gives the full-grown past is far too strong for us. Like young cats, we are blinded by the light, and still we pray for light. . . .

"Tell him his light is strong, and warm, and healthful; still we are weak, and cold, and sorry. Would he just deal out such pap as that with which he fed the Venetians and Greeks. Or even the darkness in which the Egyptians and the Children of the Sun wrought such wonders. Then we might do better. Our souls, not our eyes, require the light. Strengthen the perceptions, not the sight."

— EDWARD WALDO EMERSON

The Early Years of the Saturday Club, 1855-1870

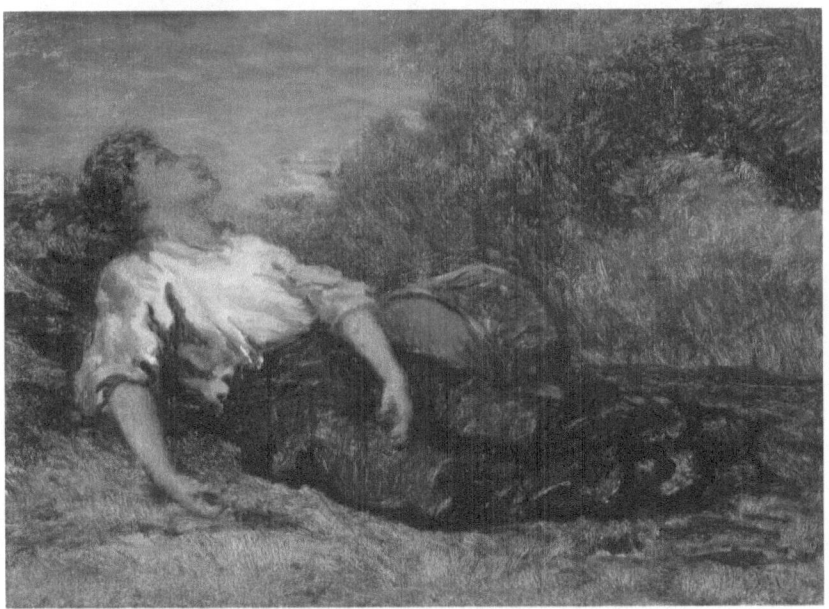

The Wounded Drummer Boy, 1862, oil, 14x19 inches, Museum of Fine Arts, Boston.

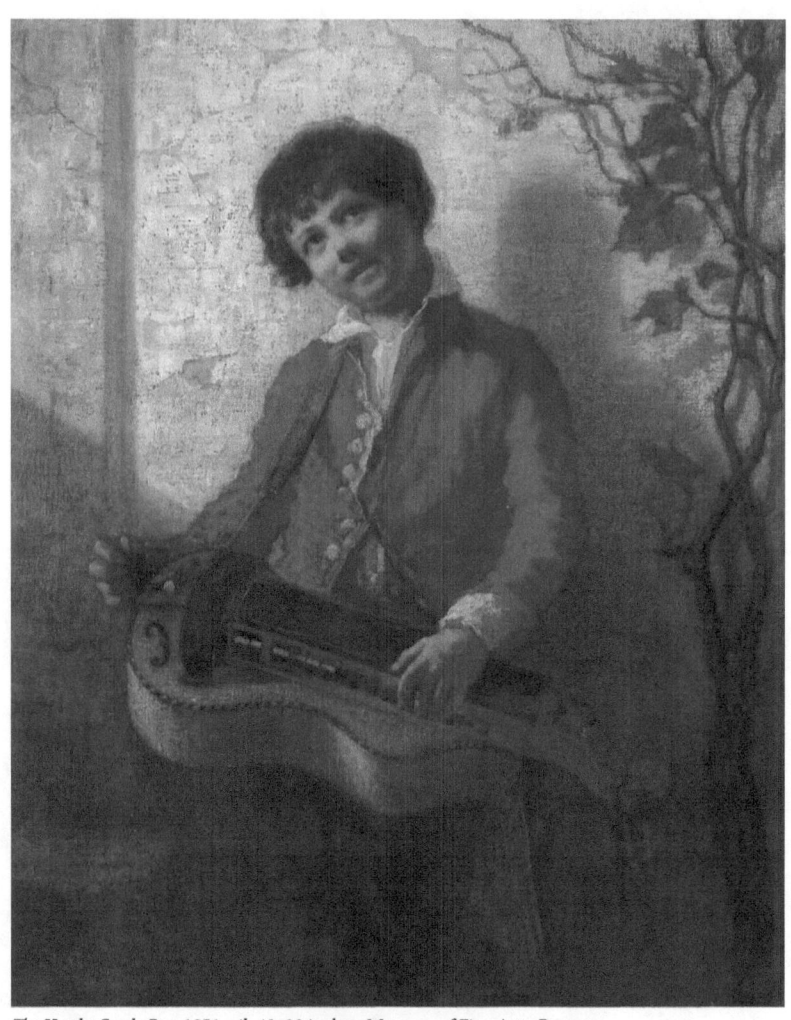

The Hurdy-Gurdy Boy, 1851, oil, 42x33 inches, Museum of Fine Arts, Boston.

INTRODUCTION

DURING A recent trip to the United States, I had the pleasure of making the acquaintance of W. M. HUNT, the great American painter, to whom I was introduced in his own *atelier* in Boston by my friend J. T. Fields. At the time of my visit he was engaged in correcting the drawings of a class of female students, and he invited me to come and look on while he continued his occupation. I was struck by the clear incisive observations which the several efforts of the students elicited as he passed them in review, and I was soon sensible that I was in the presence of a great Teacher, whose teaching, while impressed by the French training he had received in Paris, was clothed in language distinctly original, racy and American.

Miss Knowlton, the lady superintendent of this class, and herself one of HUNT's best pupils, showed me some pencil notes of his "Talks" which she had written down at odd times as he moved about amongst his pupils. I borrowed these, and looked over them quietly in the evening, and the result was that through my recommendation she obtained HUNT's consent to publish them. I believe them to contain the substance of the best practical teaching I know on the subject of Painting. Divorced from the pupil and his work, which gave them their special value, they will appear somewhat disconnected and sometimes contradictory, but to the Art student these notes will give all the information he is able to gather from the experience of a greater artist than himself.

— LOWES DICKINSON

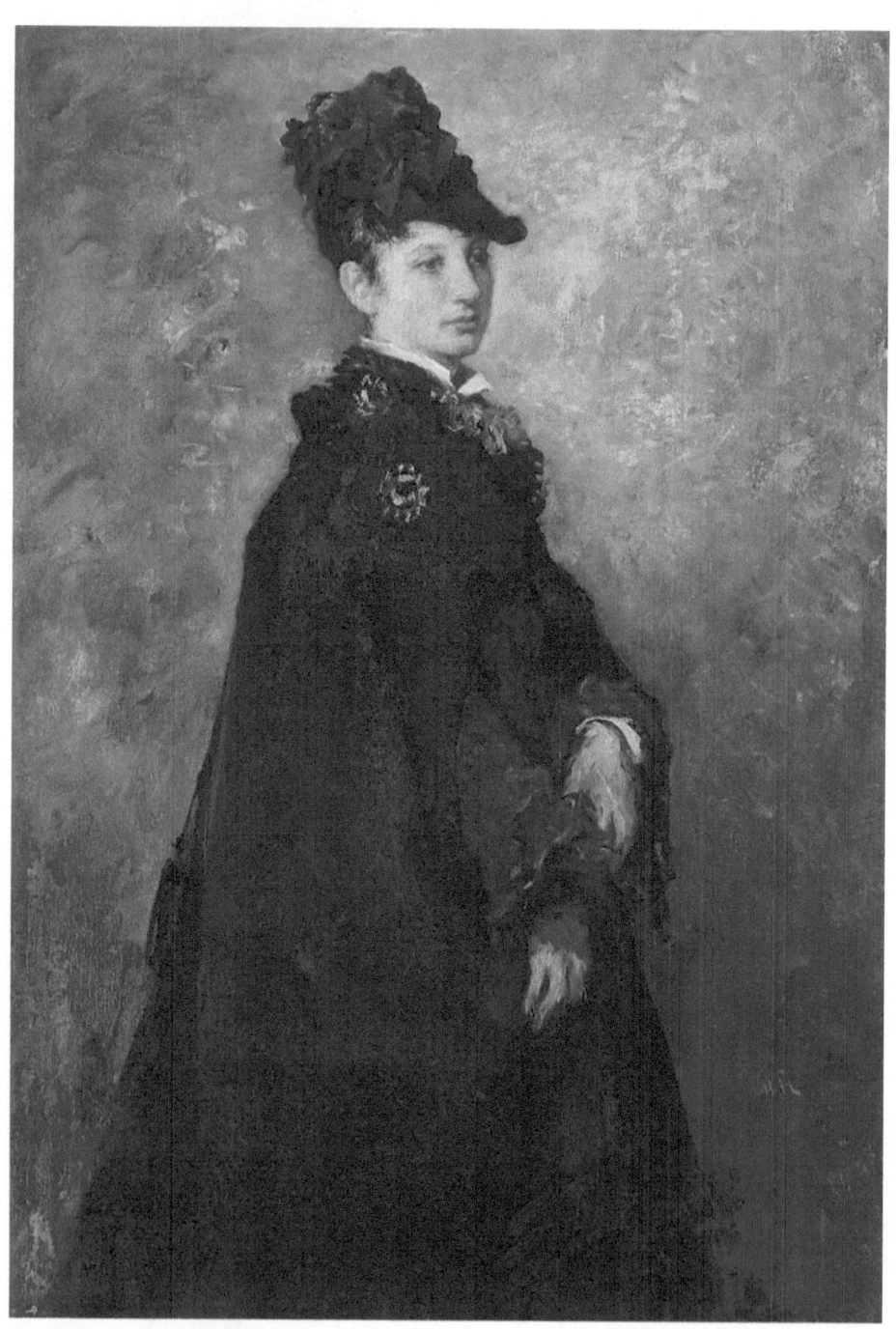

Portrait of a Lady, 1870, oil, 56x38 inches, Museum of Fine Arts, Boston.

PREFACE

THESE EXTRACTS, fragmentary and incomplete from Mr. HUNT's Instructions were jotted down on backs of canvases and scraps of drawing-paper, without knowledge of short-hand.

Their publication has been requested by artists in Europe and America.

— HELEN M. KNOWLTON

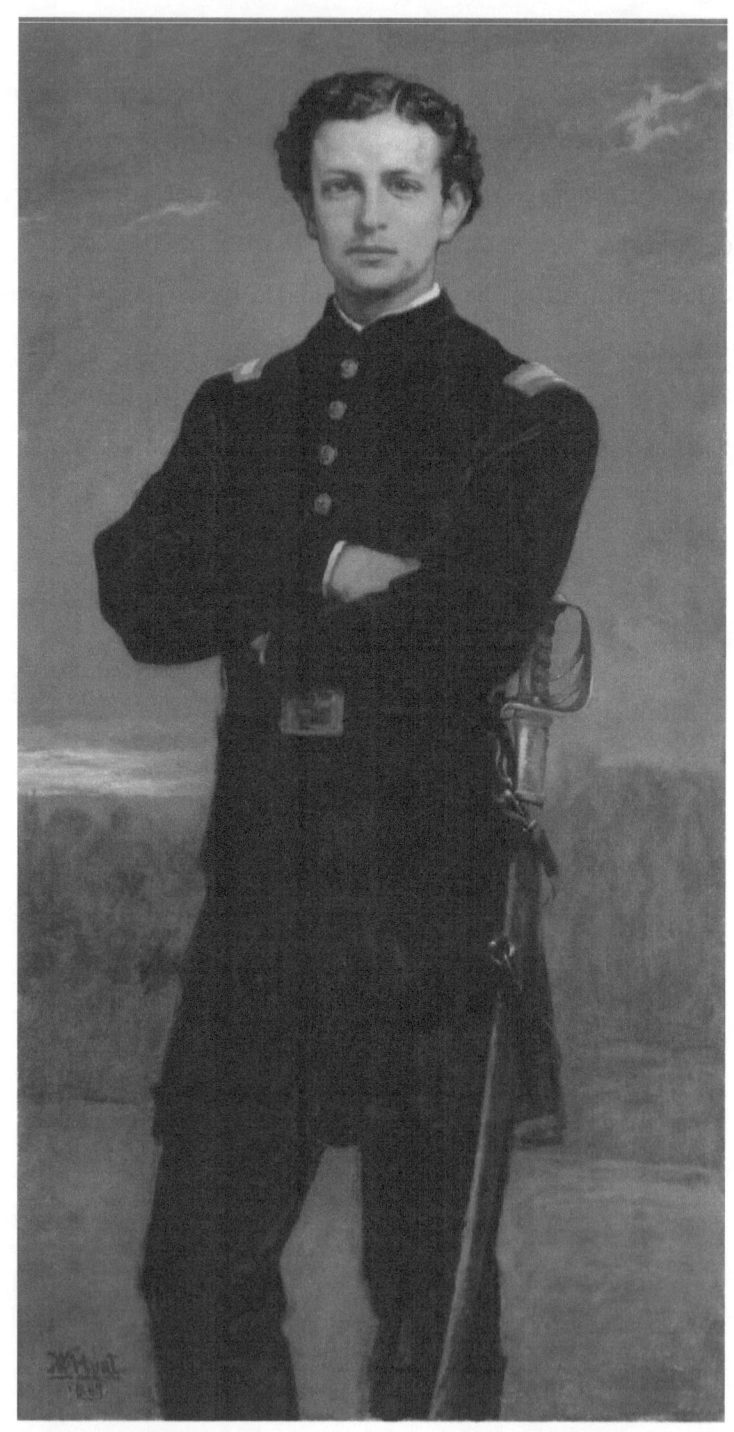

Lt. Huntington Frothingham Wolcott, 1867, oil, 61x30 inches, Museum of Fine Arts, Boston.

FORWARD

I HAVE read Hunt's notes *attentively*, and have been greatly interested in his remarks. He says vigorously a good many things we say amongst ourselves, though he appears at times to contradict himself, inasmuch as he tells a man to express himself in his own way, and at the same time it cannot be done in that way. On the *whole* his advice is undeniably sound and useful to the student, if he, the student, can possibly anticipate what comes of experience.

"The fact is, what constitutes the finest art is indescribable, the drawing not faultless, but possessing some essence beyond what is *sufficient*. The French School which Hunt speaks of appears to me at this moment to aim chiefly at perfection.[1]

"Meissonier is more complete than an old master ever was. I continually see French work of which one can only say, I don't see how it can be better, and yet it is not necessarily Fine Art of the highest order, not greater than Hogarth, who was innocent of all *finesse* of execution. The question is how hard a man hits, not how beautifully he uses the gloves: and a useful writer on Art should be able to separate the various qualities in our work without prejudice, which is one of the greatest curses we have to fight.

"I should like very much to see your friend when he comes over here and we will have an exhaustive talk on the subject. He is healthy and manly, so that there would be no *cunning* defence of his principles, which are in the main my own."

— SIR JOHN EVERETT MILLAIS R.A.

---

1. "Watteau is a striking instance of charm and grace *without* the perfection of drawing and out-of-door lighting which is obtained invariably by the best men of the French and Fortuny school"

Talks About Art

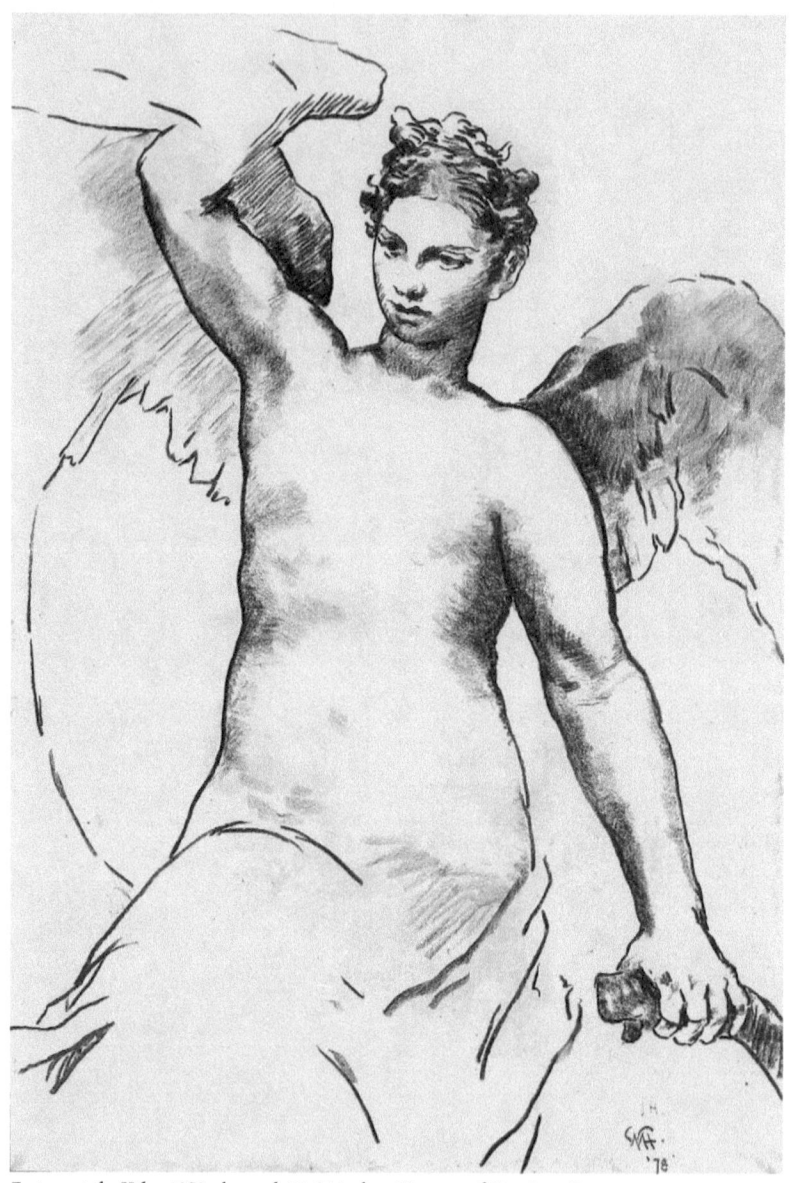

Fortune at the Helm, 1878, charcoal, 83x54 inches, Museum of Fine Arts, Boston.

Drawing?

"Yes, or *trying!*"

All anybody can do is to *try*. Nobody ever does anything! They only try!

NATURE IS economical. She puts her lights and darks only where she needs them. Don't try to be more skillful than she is!

WHY DRAW *more* than you see? We must sacrifice in drawing as in everything else.

YOU THOUGHT it needed *more* work. It needs *less*. You don't get mystery because you are too conscientious. When a bird flies through the air you see no *feathers*. Your eye would require more than one focus: one for the bird, another for the feathers. You are to draw *not reality, but the appearance of reality!*

YOU PUT in so many lights and darks that your work is mystery overdone: — a negation of fact.

YOU SEE a beautiful sunset, and a barn comes into your picture. Will you grasp the whole at once in a grand sweep of broad sky and a broad mass of dark building, or will you stop to draw in all the shingles on the barn, perhaps even the nails on each shingle; possibly the shaded side of each nail? Your fine sunset is all gone while you are doing this.

YOU ARE trying to compose without knowledge! Get your impressions from nature. Composition is simply a recollection of certain facts. No exaggeration can be stronger than Nature, for nothing is so strange as the truth. It is wilder and more weird than fancy. Look to Nature for material, and then use it as you have need. Hawthorne kept a notebook of hints which he obtained from Nature and from life; and to this he referred while writing his romances.

(Study of game with simple, flat background.) YOUR BACKGROUND is wanting in simplicity and flatness. It is not a wall; does not stay back; and the birds do not come forward. Nothing is apparent without a background.

A WHITE egg against a white paper is as nothing. It's no easy matter to paint a background. I venture to say that the old painters had more difficulty with their grounds than with their figures. You know the story of Vandyke brought to Rubens with this recommendation: "He already knows how to paint a background. That is more than I can do!" was the reply.

LOOK AT that figure, and draw it as if it were a plant. Remember that background and clothing have reference to the figure. You might change the whole drawing of the face, yes, draw in the face of another boy, without materially changing the character of the figure.

THERE IS force and vitality in a first sketch from life which the after-work rarely has. You want a picture to seize you as forcibly as if a man had seized you by the shoulder. It should impress you like reality Velázquez and Tintoretto could do this like no one else — not Titian even, whose work was beautifully modelled and coloured, but had not this quality of instantly seizing and holding the attention. I saw a man walk by. I have an impression in my brain of that man. I did not scrutinize him. I am not sure that he took steps exactly two feet and a half long. That had nothing to do with the *impression*. In your sketches *keep the first vivid impression*. Add no details that shall weaken it. Look first for the big things.

1st. Proportions.

2nd. Values — or masses of light and shade.

3rd. Details that will not spoil the beginnings.

YOU TALK about "practice of the hand." It has less to do with drawing than you think. You draw with your brain, with your eyes. You could draw with your toes, like the man in Antwerp.

Old Poussin said, "My hand trembles with old age; but I think it will yet follow the dictates of my brains."

STRIVE FOR simplicity. Not complexity. If you are going to Africa with a large cargo of merchandise, and you learn that, by reaching there on a certain day, you can double the price you were to get, throw half your cargo overboard, and arrive there in season to get your double price. Don't put needless expense into painting a head. Don't try to match tints. Rose and pearly colours blend into each other so that no one can unite them if painted separately. *Keep the impression of your subject as one thing.* Don't have the face a checkerboard of tints. Use such colours as nature uses, but not try to keep them distinct. Your work may be called monotonous; but one tone is better than many which do not harmonize.

———————

LAY ASIDE your intelligence and draw things as they look to you, no matter if you don't know what they are. Some people who wear two or three sets of spectacles draw well Now you have learned to get the masses, copy Albrecht Dürer and Hans Holbein for accuracy and form. Then draw them from memory, and thus make them a part of yourself.

———————

"I AM trying for sentiment."

"Sentiment" if you like. But do embroider it upon a possibility.

(A model in gold colour and black lace.) Aha, an omnibus in mourning!

———————

DON'T TALK of what you are "going to do." *Do It!*

———————

GIVE UP the idea of "colour" for a while. Consider masses — values, only. Some engravings of Titian's pictures almost represent his colour. At first sacrifice the beauty of your drawing to getting values.

MAKE ON a flat paper, the map of the thing. Then look for tangibility. See what makes the *picture*. The picture is what cannot be described in any other way than by painting. Literature cannot take the place of art.

ALL NOTES in music are not high. There must be low tones as well. Put in only such details as will help the masses. Don't have your work *all trills*.

HOW ARE things visible? Can you see an egg against a white background? Not by drawing a line around it can you make it evident.

THE VITALITY of flesh is *felt*. You cannot see the outline of that arm. It exists by the help of what lies next to it. The dark blue apron and the bit of blue waist help to make it visible.

LAY ON your colour like the Florentine mosaics, which are made of flat pieces joined. Keep the masses flat, simple, and undisturbed, and spend your care on skillfully joining the edges.

YOU CAN always draw as well as you know how to. I flatter myself that I know and feel more than I express on canvas; but I know that it is not so.

WHAT MAKES an eye beautiful? Not the eye itself, although

there are intrinsic forms which we acknowledge to be beautiful. It is the *regard*, the soul; and, in part, what surrounds the eye. Not the "liquid look." A snail has that.

OUR WHOLE life is given to looking at little things. We refuse to see broadly, to grasp a whole.

ONE DARK and one light place in every picture.

WE ARE not satisfied to do simply the things which we *can* do. We must draw something too hard for us. We must sing songs that have notes too high for us. How rare to hear a singer whose voice is not strained to reach impossible tones! Who wants to hear the highest tone that you can sing? We want to feel that there is a reserved force.

ELABORATION IS not beauty, and sandpaper has never finished a piece of bad work.

PICTURESQUENESS CAN be expressed in five minutes by light and shade.

IT'S THE *doing* of the thing that's important. *Doing* is bad enough: but *not doing is worse!*

YOU DONT know what persistent effort is.
Think of the violin student in the Paris Conservatoire, who

was more than a year trying to bend his thumb as he had not been taught to do in the provinces.

––––––––––

THIS DOING things to suit people. They'll hate you, and you won't suit them. Most of us live for the critic, and he *lives on us.* He doesn't sacrifice himself. He gets so much a line for writing a criticism. If the birds should read the newspapers they would all take to changing their notes. The parrots would exchange with the nightingales, and what a farce it would be!

––––––––––

SKETCH SOMETIMES by dragging the charcoal loosely over the paper, making cobweb lines.

––––––––––

I WISHED YOU all to begin by drawing that squirrel, because I wish you to *learn to record* an impression. So I have you rub in a dark shape, and then form it. After getting values and masses, work with exactness, as Holbein did. You must be able to draw a bird in charcoal so that one could not tell which is the bird and which the drawing. Must model in two colours so completely that the drawing will seem to have colour.

––––––––––

CAREFULLY MAP out your work at first. Hold up two perpendicular lines, and get the idea of *where* it will come upon the paper. With *persistent, slow carelessness, work firmly, wilfully.* Dare to make a mistake if it be a bold one. Think of the Egyptian image, with an arm longer than the whole figure, pointing, with decision and daring; and so strong that the beholder bows before it. We dare to make the letter D, but we niggle over a drawing till it is so weak that it has nothing of nature in it — only *ourselves*.

COMPARE CONSTANTLY lines and angles, now you have the idea of values. Hold a looking-glass before your model and your drawing. Take a second's glance only, and see if the impression be the same. If it be not, ask "What is the difference?" Reflect as well as work! Get a *system* of working!

"IT SEEMS as if nothing would ever come to me." Nothing *comes* into *anybody's* head. It is persistent love of a thing that tells finally. And we are helped immensely by putting down our impressions. We don't try for fear that we can't.

WHEN I WAS a little boy I wanted to learn the violin, but a certain man discouraged me. "Don't learn the violin. It's *so hard*." I could kick that man now! It is easier to eat dip-toast than to play the violin; but it doesn't meet the same want.

YOU CAN develop a child's faculties by drawing better than by books; and no other study will so quicken his perceptions. Pin-holes through a paper give a child a better idea of the stars than all the study of astronomy.

CHILDREN SHOULD learn to draw as they learn to write, and such a mystery should not be made of it. They should be encouraged, not flattered. As it is, every child shows some disposition to draw early — marking on doors, tables, books, "whole sheets of paper," — "which must not be wasted," while the parents who would save that paper, write the most vapid nonsense. With no help and encouragement, the child gradually loses its desire to draw; gets interested in other things, until the wish to draw again breaks out, and then double effort is required to get the facility which might have been gained insensibly.

————————

LET ME give you a few simple rules for learning to draw:—

First, see of what shape the *whole* thing is.

Next, put in the line that marks the movement of the whole. Don't have more than one movement in a figure ! You cannot patch parts together.

Simple lines! Then, simple values!

Establish *the fact of the whole.* Is it square, oblong, cube, or what is it? Keep in mind to look at the map of the thing! Put in all that is of greatest importance at first. It will never be the same again.

Keep things in their right places.

When values are so nearly alike that it is difficult to distinguish them, make them alike, and thus learn to simplify your masses.

————————

KEEP YOURSELF in the habit of drawing from memory. The value of memory-sketches lies in the fact that *so much is forgotten.* In time we must learn to leave out in our finished pictures these things which we now leave out through ignorance or forgetfulness. We must learn what to sacrifice.

MORE IMAGINATION is required to express a human being than to express all the dragons.

Imagination makes serpents squirm upwards, when everybody knows that they crawl upon the ground. Imagination comes in after we have had experience.

BE EARNEST, and don't worry, and you will learn twice as fast. You will some day arrive at a time when you can say, "That's *right!*" But you must learn your alphabet first.

I DON'T BELIEVE in trying to see more than you *can* see, nor in remembering more than you can remember.

IF WE would only work simply! If a bit of canvas uncovered has a better effect than it would have if paint were on it; if something half done looks better than anything finished; in a word, if the Lord helps us in that way, let us say, "Much obliged!" and take the help; and not, because *we* did not do it, think that we must work over that spot and so spoil it.

A MAN whom I am painting says of his portrait, "Very good! But here's a bit of canvas with no paint upon it." "Oh, ah, indeed." And then, to please that man, I cover that spot and spoil the best thing in the picture!

LOOK AT that hair. I say I'll paint that hair. It's brown; I know that it is brown. But then people say that my grays are nice. So I must put in some of those "nice grays." I forget nature and do so. A visitor calls. "But that hair is rather gray." "Oh, yes. Well, my light is a north light, and things look rather gray in it." And so I persuade myself that I *do not lie!*

WE MUST be true to our instincts. Shakespeare, like all great men, was true to his instincts. Bret Harte is true to his. Abraham Lincoln believed in his own instincts! And why shouldn't he, since he had the best!

THERE'S LOTS of fun in this world after all! And if there isn't there is in the next. And we're going there sure!

ART IS all that remains of man.

IF YOU could see me dig and groan, rub it out and start again, hate myself and feel dreadfully. The people who "do things easily." Their things you look at easily, and *give away easily!*

SURFACE WORK makes no impression, except that it is *prettily done.*

NOTHING IS firm but the positiveness of truth. Don't make positive lines that are not true.

MEMORY IS a mighty simple little thing, and is improved by adding *one* little thing, not shovelfuls. Could you fill a pail at Niagara. No, it must be filled by drops.

A HUNDRED times too much work is done. Get porridge enough together in one day to last two. Make a good struggle, and then rest. Kill enough game in one afternoon to last a week; otherwise, if rabbit gets a stomachache and stays at home, you starve to death.

IT IS a privilege to see *how* a thing is done, and a bore to *show* how it is done.

YOU CAN fire one bullet against another one so exactly that the two shall weld into one.

"HOW DO you do?" I don't know, and I don't care. If I did I should know.

"I CAN'T *see* anything." Don't want you to. You can *see* more than you can *do*.

DO *as well as you can!*

INSPIRATION IS nothing without work.
Look for the great lines first. You must accustom yourself to

getting proportion in a very definite way. Don't be in a hurry; and *give up all that you think you know.*

At first drawing is putting dark where dark is, in the direction in which it goes, and in comparison with other darks.

Make light lines, and use these lines as limits where the work will go.

FEAR NOT to represent impressions as Nature gives them to you !

IGNORE WHAT Nature ignores!

A CIRCUS-RIDER *must not* miss his jump! He has *got to do it!* Have seen one bite his hands to get himself up to the point!

MAKE CAREFUL tracings of photographs from the old masters, — especially from Albrecht Dürer and Montegna. Titian not firm enough.

Read Taine's "Art in Greece," and William Hazlitt's "Criticisms on Art."

WHAT WE do best is done against difficulties. Told R. H. Fuller, if being a night watchman made him paint, to continue to be a night watchman.

(An owl against a sky background.) DON'T BOTHER about the *owl*, but about the *whole* picture. Sacrifice everything to

the lights and shades. There is only one way to have light. Have darkness to make it on. Put down what you see.

Nothing exists without its background. It's *where* the bird is that makes the bird.

———————

DRAW A LINE around your sketch for a frame, and this frame gives distance.

———————

THINK ALL that you can. Put in as little hand-work as possible, and as much intelligence. Permit yourself the luxury of doing it in the simplest way.

We cannot arrive at the light and dark that there is in Nature, so we must *exaggerate,* if we can.

———————

IN DRAWING, as in pistol-shooting, pay your whole attention to the *object aimed at.* Keep your finger gently on the trigger, making it close slowly, deliberately, imperceptibly, — like fate; and, after that is started, put your whole mind upon the aim, and make everything bend to that. A bad marksman is thinking too much of the trigger. The pistol should go off itself.

———————

SOME OF YOUR older scholars must begin to settle upon some system. Find out what you like to do, and begin to do it. Every one must express something as it looks to him. When everybody is original, then life will be worth living for. A few people half dare to express themselves, and how interesting they are!

WE PUT the pedal down here and there; but twenty good draughtsmen cannot make things alike; nor is it desirable that they should. Follow your own individual taste, and somebody will appreciate it

---

"TO DRAW!" What is it to draw? Any idiot who could learn to write could learn to draw. Not to draw well; for that seems to me to require more skill than anything else in the world. More than to make a plea, or a speech in the United States Senate. And that is why criticism is so cruel. It will not take any work of art for what it is worth. It is "a little too much this, and a little too much that," when the truth is, *nothing is right.* Let Raphael and Titian draw the same nose, and their drawings will be totally unlike. *You* don't see with *my* eyes; *I* don't see with *yours.* Let each see with his own, and let his attempt to render what he sees be respected.

Some people have expressed themselves as discouraged in their expectation of finding any art in America, and have "long since ceased to hope." Let us remember that art, like jelly, has always been more easily recognized when cold. It has always existed, in all nations, and the tradition will probably not die here.

Art is not always recognized in the present. In fact, most people prefer it *canned.* There are some individuals who are farther from the present than the earth from the fixed stars; and light may eventually reach their *posterity.*

If Art depended upon literature there would never be much. The artist needs *help*. The critic should come to him in love, and ask to help him.

If we "have no art," there are more people who go to see picture galleries than who go to see libraries. There are more people today studying Greek art than there are people studying Greek literature.

The artist is an interpreter of Nature. People learn to love nature through pictures. To the artist nothing is in vain; nothing beneath his notice. If he is great enough he will exalt every subject which he treats. Who sees or hears the word Albatross, and does not think of the "Ancient Mariner?"

———————

NOTHING REMAINS of a nation but its poetry, painting, sculpture, and architecture.

———————

DON'T TRY to get the *colour* of that baby's shoulder! You'll *patch* there all your life! You can't get it by patching. You've got twenty-five different things. Represent it by a simple colour, and go on. Paint it right straight through as near as you can. Take a good-sized brush, and get something that will answer for flesh-colour.

———————

YOU WANT to learn *how to paint*. Well, we won't mind now about the colour. To arrive at colour you must first learn *how to paint;* and it isn't done by patching. Learn a simple manner of proceeding. Attack things in a broad, simple way;

and, when done, you will find certain faults of colour which you can correct — *in another picture.* I must combat your eye for colour; which is first-rate, by the way; and teach you the simple, broad manner of painting. Then your natural feeling for colour will tell later. Take, for instance, burnt sienna, white, and cobalt (brown, white, and red would do it.) Lay the colour on frankly and fully. Join the edges carefully. Don't work in the centre of things. Make flat masses of the right value and put your care into the edges. Unite them carefully. Give up the idea of getting colour by niggling. Produce it in a broad, simple way; and remember that you can't copy that exactly, and the sooner you give up the idea, the better.

———

THE PASSAGE from one tint to another is all in one tone. You've spent fifteen minutes in putting a great many tints into that face. Now spend one moment in looking at it simply and taking out nearly all that you have put in. Expand planes, instead of diminishing them. Do away with as many half-tints as you can. Expand the lights, look for the limits, and keep the gradations. Scrutiny makes you eat the whole light out of your work!

———

"I WAS TRYING to keep the reflected lights."

Reflected lights! You never saw a good picture with reflected lights. They'll come of themselves in the shadows. And don't think so much of the high light on the nose. Don't believe that a face is going to be relieved by it. Look at this Greuse. I hang it up there because it is so broadly done; but it is full of dandyism, is false in many particulars, and lights are put in where light could not possibly fall. There's the same trouble in my sketch there, near it. Look at that cheek. It comes out like a sausage. I did it, I am willing to confess, and I hate it!

———————

LOOK FOR the broad lights. Don't let half-tints encroach upon them. Keep them frank. You think there's a dark here and a dark there, and you get it over-modelled. This comes from having overdone a hundred things without looking to see what the thing really is. You can't relieve the nose by putting a light upon it. You must put a shadow by the side of it.

———————

WORK AS long as you know what to do. Not an instant longer.

———————

BE CAREFULLY careless!

———————

TRY TO GET flat, even surfaces. People who paint for a living, house-painters, etc., always get flat surfaces. They don't stop to niggle.

———————

"How SHALL I paint that background?"

Go to Cambridge to find out. Literature will tell you. There is no language in art but that of the eye. Art cannot describe colour. That is the fun of picture books. They don't *say* anything.

———————

How to do it? Well, if you must know, paint it a dark, deep, invisible, olive grey.

PAINTING IS appreciation of the form, character, and colour of the things. Not oil or varnishes.

THE EYES are never alike, except in an idiot — in whose face the movement of the mouth is alike on both sides. So we need not feel bad if one corner of the mouth is up more than the other, or one eye higher than the other. However, we'll say nothing against the idiots. In another world they may be just the right kind. They are interesting sometimes, — so entirely natural.

"I DON'T KNOW about the mouth! Who does?"

MODEL THE eyebrow as if there were no colour or hair upon it. Make it look like a rivulet running over a stone. The eye is not a thing drawn flatly upon the face. What lies above and below the eye helps to make it.

THE MOUTH is not a *slit*. It is shaped like a *trumpet*. Like something through which sound may come.

"I WANT to get the look of innocence!"

Get the mouth first and the innocence afterwards; or it will be *too innocent!*

VERTICAL AND horizontal lines are unerring guides to perspective. You can draw anything with them.

GO STRAIGHT ahead and get the *likeness!* Then try to make it fascinating afterwards.

CONTINUALLY WALK away from your work, and see if your representation realizes your idea of the subject.

YOU CAN'T learn by studying Nature alone. Copy Albrecht Dürer! Look at Titian! People are afraid if you go abroad, or look at anything but Boston Common, that you'll paint like Titian or Claude.

You couldn't learn geography or algebra without books to refer to. You can't do a fine thing without having seen fine examples. I should like to see Adam draw that drapery. He'd "slip up"; you know that he would.

IT IS WORTH while to have done one thing as well as you know how; that is, to have made a careful study of an object, for the sake of seeing how a *little* thing adds.

DON'T BE entirely discouraged because you can't paint like "Pinxit" in one afternoon. It is not wholly our fault because we can't paint. It is because we have not *seen* enough!

"GETTING ALONG without instruction!"

Nobody ever did well without learning from those who had had opportunity to know what was good and great. Michelangelo, Titian, Raphael, were they "self-taught?"

I *"rather guess"* not!

I RESPECT everything that *is, because it is.* I don't respect what isn't, just because it *isn't.*

Paint for fun! I don't care whether it succeeds or not. Let success come along afterwards.

DRAW FIRM, and be jolly!

THAT SKETCH is smart, but I don't like it. It was done too hurriedly. It shows too much ambition to do a thing quickly. I don't care how badly a sketch is painted if it looks as if you really wanted to do it. I would keep you from getting too smart all at once. It would be impossible to go on with that sketch. There's the *end* of it. I repeat that it is smart, but you get there too soon. No use getting ahead of *yourself!*

I THINK THAT anything you paint ought to give the impression of an aspiration. If you hear a stutterer trying to express himself, you sympathize with him in what he wants to say.

What if you do use bad grammar! I don't care — if you have *something to say!*

No one ever did a good thing without thought, without respect. I believe in laying out just so much earnestness. What if Michelangelo had done his work in the Sistine Chapel easily?

An artist, calling one day upon Grisi, found her upon a sofa, weary and forlorn. He expressed his surprise at her appearance, declaring that she was the one mortal whom he had envied, such was her strength, buoyancy, and joyousness. He had not thought she could find life a burden. "Ah," said she, "I save myself all day for that one bound upon the stage! Not for worlds would I leave this sofa, which I must keep all day that I may be ready for my work at night" She sacrificed everything in life for that!

I saw Blondin after he had walked across Niagara on a rope, and he told me that there was not one man in the great crowd assembled to witness the feat who could even carry his balancing pole the same distance upon level ground, *as he carried it,* perfectly balanced.

Don't be careless for an instant. You know there are musicians who will not touch a piano which makes a false sound. You may call them whimsical, but they are right. You want a little rub-a-dub this evening, and are annoyed at "those particular fellows who cannot play upon a piano which is not *just right.*" Why, what would you think of your hostess, who at an evening party should say, "Now let us see you draw. We want to see you do it." Or, "Come write a little poetry. We want to see how you look when you write poetry."

———————

WHATEVER BEAUTY there is comes not by itself, but by what is around it. Take intrinsic beauty and you can multiply or subtract from it by the position in which it is to be placed. Do not devote one single instant to putting down what you don't see. You clinch at a habit which will render drawing impossible.

———————

Think — one moment out of five hundred.
Think! And believe that it requires some brains to draw.

———————

DON'T DENY the impression that you receive.

———————

YOU CAN'T finish anything until it is done. Try to finish at first, and you are digging a well up in the air!

———————

WHAT IS Drawing? How is the object visible? Difference of values produces the "effect."

———————

YOU THINK it an insult to put a shadow upon a face. The Lord doesn't think so!

———————

THAT'S A GOOD sketch. But don't touch the head again. You would spoil it. Because you have been *smart*, don't try to be *superhuman!*

I DO NOT see you walk away from your work enough! You can learn more in four minutes in that way than you could in an hour at your easel.

To *finish*, stop *fooling* over your work. Don't blister it all over with *facts. Facts are not poetry.* And stop this eternal going back to correct. I remember to have heard a distinguished statesman read aloud a French letter; and instead of reading on, to the best of his ability, he went back, correcting himself, and snubbing the words he had mispronounced; and the consequence is, that I've forgotten the substance of the letter, and only remember his blunders and corrections. I like to hear French read well; but I don't like to hear it *practised.* Demosthenes did not practise before his audiences. He did that in a cave.

It is the subjection of one thing to another that makes the picture. We want the finish of a clean, round bullet, rather than that of a chestnut burr. We don't want the finish that rats give to cheese. After they've finished it, there's nothing left.

Avoid certain petty, trivial details which people call "finish." They are of the nature of things with which one would confuse a child, deceive a fly, or amuse an idiot!

SOME SPEAK of a picture as having "certain fine points." So has a chestnut burr; and it is no compliment to a work of art to be thus spoken of. What would you think if you heard Beethoven's

Sonatas described as having "certain fine points?"

DON'T BE TOO difficult with yourself. One's self can't stand it! It discourages production. Go ahead. Produce. Produce, and don't stop to *judge* till the *last* sample has appeared. The horses which have won four-mile races have never stopped at the end of the first mile to criticise their own pace. Others will do this; and whatever others will attend to, leave them behind to attend to it!

I think it is the safest place to be in, viz.: the place *just ahead* of where one is being attacked!

Let the critic and the historian fumble in carrion, but *a producer should always he in the present*. The *next* work is the one in which to put all the good, and to leave out some of the bad of the past.

But never attack one's own drawings. Poor things, they can't defend themselves. *Acknowledge only*; and *go on*.

Apropos of criticizing one's own work, I am sure that, if the best hen in the world, after laying an egg, looked around long enough — criticizing it, not a chicken would ensue. But in laying, ever laying, and sitting, ever sitting, the hen throws all the responsibility upon the chickens.

IN PAINTING those flowers make first a neutral tint, preserving the values. Then dash in the colour of the flower. In that way you get a red or yellow tint which is agreeable, instead of red or yellow *paint*, which would be offensive.

IN DRAWING that white azalea, make the petals in light, as distinct as if they were cut with a stencil.

"WON'T THAT picture crack!"

I don't care if it does. It would be better if more pictures cracked. Garrets are as essential as galleries. There must be a place in which to put bad work; and the more garrets, the more things get sifted.

DON'T TURN the head one way, and the eyes another. The eyes always lead the movement of the head except when we are listening. Look at me. There, that's what you're trying to do.

It *isn't* becoming.

Hang the "becoming." It isn't *natural.*

YOU ARE longing to get something which is in your own mind; not looking to see what is before you.

TRY TO get the luminous quality of that face in the light. It is a very simple, neutral colour. Its beauty is in its gradations.

You haven't yet a belief in the fact that *the simple mass of light is never troubled with shadows.* You put in that shadow because you thought it would help you to get "relief." *Look for the relief of the whole.*

OUR EYES are trained to scrutiny from childhood. We are

all looking for holes in people's elbows, and dust on their coat-collars. It is the mean, ordinary way of looking at human nature. We who paint must not use our eyes *so* because they *can* be so used. If the coat *is* greasy it may be beautiful when painted.

———————

LOOK FOR a realization of what you want. Don't go at things to approximate. Ask yourself positively the definition of the thing before you. What is it? Of what colour is it? What colour and form is nearest to it?

Make a little frame with your hand, and look through it See what your *picture* is, and paint it in frankly. Put it in as you think it ought to be when left.

———————

WHERE IS your *silk* dress that is going to touch the sobriety of that old woollen gown? That apron is not neat, but it suggests neatness.

———————

DON'T PUT a face upon that baby which looks like Demosthenes, or like a judge in a courtroom!

———————

IF we can *do what we see,* and get our perceptions up by seeing fine things that have been done, it wouldn't be necessary to have such very fine models as we think.

We don't work enough for the sake of learning, but too much for the sake of having it known that we work. The desire to excel is natural and commendable, but we must cut it down, and *sacrifice ourselves,* in order to learn.

You ARE so desirous to do the thing that you don't look to see what it is. If you could learn how to do certain things from looking at fine works, it would seem possible to do well constantly.

"It isn't quite right!"

Of course it isn't, and it can't be. No matter. Push on! You mustn't expect to do anything perfectly. Do as well as you can, and let it go. If a streetcar horse makes a miss-step the driver doesn't say, "Here. Go back. Do that over again." No; go ahead continually!

A MODERN portrait-painter told his sitter that when his portrait had become mellowed by time it would have the same tone that Titian's work had. He forgot that there were a great many painters who lived at the same time as Titian whose works do not at all resemble his.

No, it is a mistake to believe that colours used now do not last as well as those used in the times of the old masters. The truth is, that those men *knew how to paint*. They worked frankly and didn't niggle. They let their pictures alone, and didn't fool over them.

Don't CONSIDER it a "duty" to exaggerate the *plainness* only. Exaggerate the *beauty* if you can. Hang the "duty." Try to do the thing *as you see it*. Don't think of making a handsome picture. Try to represent the reality, and it will be handsome enough.

———

You can only give out what you receive.

———

"In painting this head, how shall I Join the tones?"

Don't ask *me*. *I* don't know how. If I could find out, how, I would go ten million miles on my knees to do it! We all want to know how things are done. Boston is a great place for receipts. There is a receipt for being scientific, one for being sentimental, another for being religious. But painting is something for which you can't get a receipt; so people say that their teachers are to blame, that they "don't impart enough."

———

"What colours should you have used?" The colours for me to use are not the colours for you to use. If I had made that sketch I probably should not have got such a clear colour in the forehead. You get first-rate *parts* of things, but the great thing is *to get the relation of parts*. Outsiders would say that the face is covered with moth-patches; but I say that it is real earnest work. True colour, and like life.

Strive for cool colour in flesh. For colour like that of tea-roses. The old fellows used cool colours. Nothing snuffy about them.

Work while your brain is full of the picture before you. Don't bother and worry, and don't gloat over it, until you have wholly lost your first impression. When your interest slips away a little, quit your sketch; go and read a newspaper, for instance. Forget all about it. Then approach it from a distance, and your fresh eyes will tell you where you are in your work.

———————

You MUST get over the idea that the only firm thing is a fine line. Firmness is consistency, solidity — something thicker than a line. Why, an infant's cheek may be firm. A firm man doesn't go in a line. He is firm throughout. Firmness is in thickness as much as in outline. A hard outline on the edge looks thin and weak rather than firm. A hoop is not a firm thing.

———————

FIND THE middle of the figure, and then hold up vertical and horizontal lines across it. See what parts come under the same line.

Use your canvas as you would a slate — with the idea that you can rub out and add and subtract at will. Always have plenty of canvases at hand. It is a luxury to know that you have twenty-five or thirty ready to do with as you please.

———————

TRANSPARENT WORK in drawing doesn't amount to anything. Get a good solid tone. That crisscross of lines doesn't mean anything, unless it is a snow-storm. If you want black, make it black. If you want white, make it white. Don't be afraid of getting it black if black is what you want. You'll never get anything as long as you live if you don't take a broad piece of charcoal, or a big brush, and make a good solid tone — where there is one. Instead of one white light in your sketch, you have fifty.

———————

(Sketch of a little boy in red stockings.) THE STOCKINGS were

painted with Prussian blue and white at first; then a red tint given to them. If they had been painted red at once, the red would have been too glaring. It would have been a picture of red stockings.

———————

THE STRUGGLE of one colour with another produces colour.

———————

THE HIGHEST light on the face is usually on the spot which would get wet first if you were out in the rain.

———————

MAKE THE TINT on the cheek uniform and flat You spoil it by over-modelling. There is no half-tint on the light side of the nose. It is the same as the cheek. Make it flat, and it will be round enough.

———————

IN TRYING to paint sunlight behind those trees, bang away, and get it *light enough*. "What colour to use?" I don't care what colours you use, only g*et it light where it is light.*

———————

I AM ALWAYS hoping to be able to paint a portrait in one day. There's my sketch — my impression of the boy as he came for the first time into the studio. With a few lines I represented my idea of his figure, manner. *My* impression, I say. Not yours: not the impression of anybody else. No one else would have sketched him in *just* that way.

Now don't think that when I say I want to paint him in one

day that I count it only one day's work. For weeks I hare considered it, have prepared different grounds — four certainly; have experimented on similar grounds to know which will be the best. I've thought of it day and night. Awaking at three o'clock in the morning with the thought of whether I can get him vigorous enough against a certain background. So I keep this picture in mind until I feel that I can strike the right colour here, there; I can make this dark enough, that light enough. Then, when the time comes, I must be ready to paint; and I tell you it's no joke to paint a portrait. I wonder that I am not more timid when I begin. I feel almost certain that I can do it. It seems very simple. I don't think of the time that is sure to come when I almost despair; when the whole thing seems hopeless. Into the painting of every picture that is worth anything, there comes some time, this period of despair!

———————

ASK YOURSELF positively what is the realization of the thing. If the line is straight, make it so as nearly as possible at once. If it is crooked, make it positively crooked. Lay down palette and brushes, and ask, as if your life depended upon it, what is the colour? Decide, as nearly as you can, what will make it, and do it at once. Don't be "wabbling" all the morning, and approximate in the afternoon!

———————

GIVE UP the habit of working with charcoal in lines. Make the surface solid; either light or dark. Don't have your background look like a snow-storm. Rub down a smooth surface,

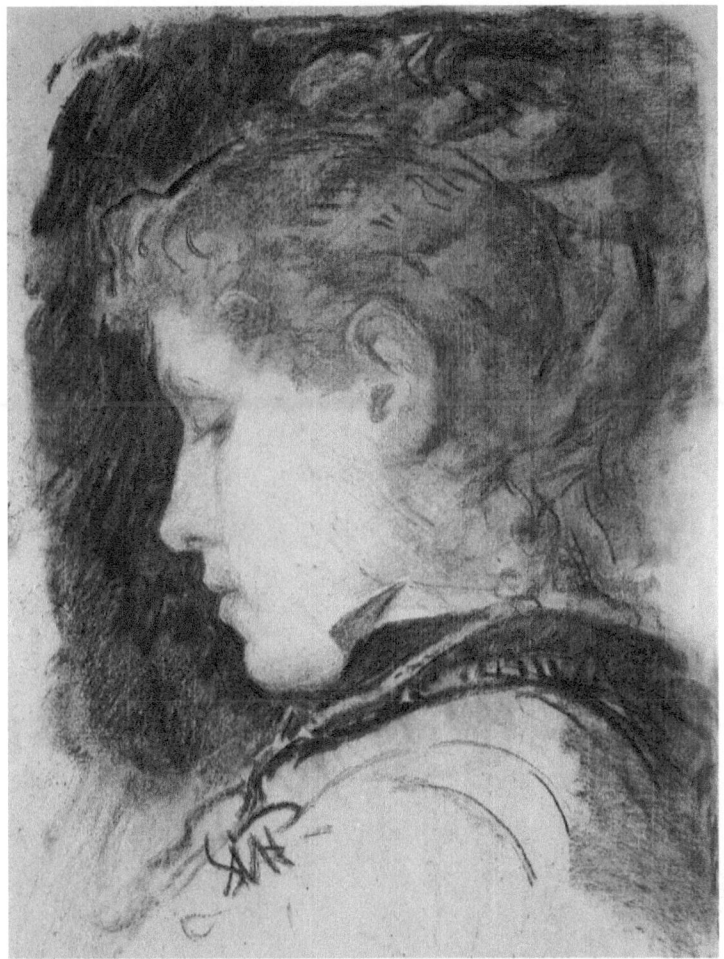

Portrait of a Lady, 1870, charcoal on laid paper, 18x12 inches, Museum of Fine Arts, Boston.

and draw the head firmly against it. Put dark where you see dark, and light where you see light. If you are looking at the braid in that hair you do not see the whole head. Do little things after establishing the great masses.

You get a habit of pat, patting little lines that don't mean anything. Don't make lines until you think you know where they belong. Then go ahead

Don't work headlessly. Criticise occasionally what you have done, instead of keeping closely at work. If your hand is always on your paper you will work thoughtlessly. There's nothing there that you can't render in ten minutes. Don't check yourself by over-anxiety. Put down frankly what you believe. Put it down as you think it is, and it will be a great deal nearer right than if done in any other way.

IN PAINTING the stem of a flower, put your brush in the right place, and draw it down at once, firmly. Don't go along tick, tick, tick, and don't be afraid of it!

IN USING water-colours try to get fulness of vigour as you would with oil colours. Don't hesitate to get it "awfully" coloured. I would go, at once, to the fullest extent that my palette would allow. I would try, once or twice, to see how vigorous I could get it .

"WOULD YOU paint Mr. A ——, if I could persuade him to sit for his portrait?"

I don't like *persuaded* sitters. I never could paint a cat if the cat had any scruples, religious, superstitious, or otherwise, about sitting.

"I FELT LIKE doing it; but I thought it was my duty to do differently; so I was trying to."

Do as you feel. Hang duty — in drawing and painting. Duty never painted a picture nor wrote a poem, nor built a fire. *Do it as it seems to you to be.*

PUT IN what you need to express the tiling. *Everything* is beautiful! That's what's the matter. People wouldn't see the beauty of this floor, with its light and shade and colour. They would only see dirt and spots.

LOOK AWAY from your work. Don't be for ever looking at your own work. And you are trying too much for tone, tone, tone. You've got to deny that *that is that,* for *it isn't that!* Look at that drawing. It is more like life than your painting. Why the paper is nearer the colour of the model than your work. People don't know how little it takes to make that colour. It is made of nothing. It is almost black and white. A drawing comes mighty near nature when you mind all the values.

I LIKE THAT drawing because the paper is *completely filled.* That is the beauty of the Greek coins. They are completely filled. They fill the space that they occupy.

A QUARTER of an inch is enough to disengage eternity on.

DON'T UNDERPAINT too heavily. I don't believe in so much *loading.* What is it? It is making a great mass of dirty colour which is of no use to yourself or anybody else. Underpaint simply, and with no unnecessary "body." Then a little colour tells in your next painting, which, by the way, must not be undertaken immediately. Let it stand a year if possible, until you have forgotten it. Then pull it out and go on with it. Long drying seems to induce some chemical change, which helps you in finishing your picture. Titian preferred to let his first painting stand six or eight months. I tell you, those old fellows *knew!*

You're all in such a hurry to learn to paint. Why, I've been at it all my life, and I don't today feel that I know anything. I'm not sure that I can go on with a single one of these portraits that I've begun.

You say that I told you yesterday to work in one way, and that today I tell you to work in another. Certainly; and tomorrow I shall probably suggest a third, if I think by "tacking ship" you can make headway.

Don't hesitate to leave a point wherein you are strong, and to strengthen yourself in a direction wherein you are weak. Then return with freshness, and carry your strong point along.

By being always careful you will gradually lose all freedom of movement, and come eventually to use only the tips of your fingers. A cat don't catch a mouse with her claws alone. She strikes out from her shoulders, after making a bound from her hind feet.

You must necessarily spoil a good deal of paper. Therefore, I beg of you, spoil it cheerfully. You will learn freedom of movement in so doing. If a child were as pedantic and fussy in his endeavours to pronounce as we are in trying to exactly determine certain little forms and colours, he would never learn to speak.

You might as well expect to learn to shoot by firing off one grain of powder at a time. No ! Fire off the whole charge, right or wrong! The direction may be faulty at firsts but the bullet will take effect somewhere, visibly ; and if in the wrong place, *vary your aim, but not the power.*

———————

STRIKE FRANKLY and strong from your convictions, and your faults will be much more easily corrected; for they will be the more evident. If you use only your finger-tips you will acquire a stiff wrist, elbow, shoulder, and back.

Convince yourself of the general form of an object. Swing the whole form upon your paper or canvas. Then amuse yourself by dividing it and subdividing it by details. Make your hulk first. Then step the masts, and, if you like, add a pennon. Never try to hang a head upon a nose.

———————

I KNOW THAT the oak grows from the acorn, but the acorn contains the oak. Wing a chrysalis, and you have a butterfly. Add legs and head to the form of an egg, and you have at least one chicken, but you can't make one with a ticking full of feathers.

You can't even see a hair on a cat without losing sight of pussy.

When the tree throws off its leaves it doesn't give up the right to appear in one simple form or mass against the sky— except to the squirrel, who only deals with one branch at a time.

The Greek sculptors did not spend any *more* time than we do on the hair of their dogs and horses, and yet —— !

At any rate, put off this kind of work until the last, and if you should by any chance forget it, your friends will certainly remind you of it. *The want of an eyelash or a button never goes unnoticed.*

Therefore, first be sure that you have accomplished the bulk,—that is, roundness and thickness of your object; for should you fail in this, the critic might not observe the want of it, and it would go for ever unexpressed.

In other words, *do as does nature*. Hide the solid form of the figure under the folds of the clothing; and never run the risk of undertaking to render the form and movement of the bird after you have completed the feathers!

Chase your shadow, — *but don't run after originality.*

Should you grow discouraged at your slow progress, try for a year or two to play a violin solo!

When an inexperienced person discourages you by not liking your work, ask yourself how many dollars you would give for his opinion.

"WHAT SHALL I do to soften the face?"

Oh, take yellow, red, and blue and white, and do what your *feelings* tell you to do. Words don't help you. I might as well tell you how to write a poem by handing you a number of letters, and saying, "There I use these thus and so, and a poem will come of it." You would answer, "But that wouldn't be what I wish to say." Therefore you must pick out your own letters, and write your own poem.

"WILL YOU please to correct some of the mistakes in my work?"

Mistakes, we *go on by mistakes!* Get ahead by making them. Just as a crab, to make progress, walks backward.

INSTEAD OF *one* canvas ready to paint on, you ought to *have forty, and paint for a joke.* I have a hundred and fifty in waiting, and each of you ought to have ten at least. You always have gloves to wear. You need canvases just as much.

"MY THINGS get to look so like monkeys, that I am afraid I am fast becoming a Darwinian."

You're behind the times. *Going* to be one. Why, I should suppose you had always been one. For a long time I've been taking that for a starting-point. Now I believe that some of us are going back to the monkey state. Part of the race are going *from* it, and part *towards* it!

I'VE JUST finished this little sketch, painting it in twenty minutes, with the intention simply of getting light in a sky. When I left it, I thought, "The first person who comes in will say, 'Oh, trying to paint like Corot!'" I wasn't trying to paint like any one: but I know that when I look at nature I think of Millet, Corot, Delacroix, and sometimes of Daubigny. Just as if we were to write a line of poetry that hit the nail sharp upon the head, it *might* make us *think of Shakespeare*.

WORK IS a stimulus to work, and loafing is a stimulus to laziness!

YOUR DRAWING is too vapory. It needs to be made definite by certain lines which you might use to disengage the head from the background. Draw a line firmly under that chin, and then you can work up to it, and lose it if you don't like it. Your work doesn't "carry" across the room. It looks like nature when you come close to it; but it must look like nature as soon as you enter the door.

You can't *literally* reproduce it, but you must use means to make it count for what you wish to represent. When Paul Veronese painted his pictures, he knew where they were to be seen. Some of them were as long as this room, forty feet perhaps. When you come near to them you might find what you would call "faults"; but I tell you that *he knew why he made use of these means*. You may say that he was "too much this, and too much that;" but ho has shown us how to make certain effects possible.

You must take for granted the experience of people who have *had* experience, and who knew what they were about. Paul Veronese will always be known as a great painter; and until we get to be greater than he, we must believe that he was right. So with Michelangelo. You may say that he distorted the muscles; that he exaggerated certain parts at the expense of others. He, like Veronese, never made a touch that he didn't need. You must see his pictures in the place in which they belonged. You can't judge altogether of paintings by photographs from them. For instance, certain lines would be made of red — which would photograph black; and you would see them dark where they were not intended to be dark.

Paul Veronese says that "art is conventional." It is not literal; any more than poetry. Titian acted upon the same idea.

"But in a very different manner ?"

Only that his name began with a T instead of a V. When he saw that his things did not count at a distance, he knew what to do to get the effect. He took *his* way; Veronese *his* way. Looking at Leonardo da Vinci, I feel that I wouldn't have done this, and I wouldn't have done that; but — *he knew!*

The Greek sculptors had their way of getting what they wanted. When the Greeks doubled a movement, they did it to strengthen a group. They sustained things to get breadth. You often see single horses painted whose legs would hardly carry their weight. You can't snap off the leg of a horse in the Parthenon!

We have got to haye faith in the biggest people that have ever done anything. If we can find out a way of doing our work with less expense, all right. Paul Veronese gives you the résumé of a thing. Velázquez painted hands with two strokes of the brush. Near the canvas you would say that his hands had but three fingers each; but, at the distance at which they were meant to be seen they were real hands?

Now it would be very easy for me to say "Yes" to your admiration of painters who are not the greatest; and it isn't what might be colled "pleasant" for me to combat your ideas. But, in spite of what you may think of me, I have a firm conviction that you haven't the true idea of *great Art!* Besides, I want to tell you that you haven't a right, at the age of twenty years, to pronounce judgment on these great artists, who may never be equalled, *never can be excelled.*

I have disliked pictures so much that I afterwards found were good, that I want to hint to you that you may, some day, want an outlet from the opinions you now hold.

The fact is, we must take, in the works of these men, what you call *faults*, and ask ourselves if they were not perhaps, *qualities.*

What a time has been made over Michelangelo's "Moses" with his horns. Michelangelo felt that Moses *must have horns!* To represent him he must have something more than a man with a full beard, and you must accept these horns just as you would a word which some poet had felt the need of, and had coined. As Michelangelo was the greatest creator that ever worked in art, hadn't we better decide that we'll wait fifteen minutes before passing judgment upon him, or upon what he did."

There was the same talk about his plan of St Peter's Church. Everybody had always raised such a hue and cry about it, comparing it unfavorably with St Paul's. Horace Binney Wallace, the Philadelphia writer upon art, was the first man to say, "Hold on. Let's look at it from the artist's point of view. Let's walk out of Rome and see it thirty miles off." This church was intended to be a sort of handle to the city. In the position which it holds, it needed to be built just as it was built

Ah, these great men! Their life was one prayer. They did nothing but their work; cared only for what they were doing, and how little the world knows of them!

Whoever really knew the Sistine Chapel decorations until photographs brought them to us. Formerly, we looked at what seemed the great brown patches, straining our eyes in the glare of light, or holding a looking glass in our hand to reflect them. They had to be brought to us before we could know them.

We must believe that *there was something in the Past*. The past has produced Homer, Shakespeare, and Michelangelo. Don't give a judgment upon them before you are ready. No use in shutting up your future. Leave it open so that you *can believe.*

Go to Europe and stay five year's; and I'll bet you a hundred thousand dollars that you'll prefer a Mantegna to a Ribera. So with Velázquez. He won't hit you at first; but later. You'll begin with Murillo and end with Velázquez!

To come down to our own time. Fifteen years ago everybody

said Delacroix was a fool. Couldn't represent what he wanted to without his peculiar crisscross work of hatching. What of it? Try to work simply; but *get what you want!* Crisscross, sit on it, pour an ink bottle over it. Only *get it!* Do as did Benvenuto Cellini. Take all your vases and recast them, in order to make your last work what you want to make it!

Five years ago scarcely a Boston individual would look at Corot. Twenty years ago nobody in Europe would buy him. He was "so peculiar." So was Christopher Columbus. *The pioneer is always peculiar!*

Paul Veronese has more qualities as a *painter* than any man who ever lived. Our idea of making a "faultless" thing is all nonsense.

Make the thing! Stick in the faults. A man's nose may be too long; but it belongs to him, and God made it. Until we get to rendering a thing, we don't see all its merits. We all like the floor of this studio better than we used to, because we've found out that we can't paint it. So of a mud-puddle. We see the beauty when we find that we can't begin to render it

The longer you dig at a thing, the more margin you will give to people who have given their lives to one pursuit

Take Millet's "Sheep Shearer." You would say that the line around the arm was too strong. But it was needed. Without it, the drawing would have been vapory. A week after the picture was done — as I thought, as anybody would have thought — I saw him digging upon it, not for pay, although he was nearly starving, but to carry it where he knew it ought to go.

We might as well say that the Egyptians were wrong in putting long arms on their figures. No, they did it with a purpose. In their sculptures you will find beautiful faces, beautiful throats, but hands without action. They believed not in action, but in repose.

There was Poussin, a lovely old chap. How the critics were down on him when he painted "Moses striking the Rock." The owner wrote him, "I don't like it! Here's a lake, made in a single moment. You've been trivial, I don't want your picture !" To which came the calm reply, "Don't worry. I thought if Moses was going to strike a rock, he might as well strike where there had once been a fountain. He knew what he was about."

Believe that those old fellows who happened to have existed have loved the thing better than we ever shall. *They stood by and dug!* Velázquez had a facility because he painted ten thousand pictures; and, furthermore, he took an oath *Never to do anything without Nature before him!* He hired a boy to stay with him, and when he wanted him he was always at hand.

IF I WERE to show that sketch of mine to some people they would say, "It looks as if you had *daubed stuff* around upon that canvas." I should feel tempted to say that they *might* "daub stuff" around, and not get so much of a picture as that even! I am trying, first of all, to get a simple, luminous colour. I don't want to make it like the colour of any *painted* sky that I ever saw. I want, I say, a simple, luminous colour.

Don't bother too much about colour. Get the effect of light, and you won't miss colour. I know that my pictures are said to "lack colour;" but I don't like a great many things which people admire for their "colour."

(*Moonlight.*) You DON'T have to be literal to a line to make an impression. Moonlight pictures are apt to look as if you had dipped the thing in ink, and half washed it out. This sketch looks like *one thing*, instead of sixteen — which is one good quality.

IN POETRY and painting, *facts do not amount to much.* Fact didn't make a Hamlet. Facts change; but ideas don't. Every seven years there is a new notion about eating eggs. One while, *soft-boiled* eggs are the thing; then *hard-boiled* eggs. Human nature continues unchanged.

The Chinese maxim, "Love your friends and be just to your enemies" remains. The Christian idea, noble and high although it is, doesn't replace the truth that it isn't in human nature to love our enemies. It is impossible. Not human. "*Love your* enemies!" — DO *it!* Don't *say* so!

A painter will often do a thing to build up a weak side, and to get an equilibrium. The critic should believe that he has a reason for what he does. Not that I want everybody to think as *I* do. Only those that want to. We don't want everybody to take "Hostetter's Bitters."

The fact is, painting is not intended for rules; but to represent something which you see and feel. There's more of the science of a picture in that sketch than in ninety-nine of the things that are called "finished." Can't do that by being an idiot. There's a cat's back that fire will come out of in a cold day; and there are a good many cats drawn that you couldn't get a spark out of.

———————

LOOKING FOR colour, and painting, are as different as fish and fishing.

———————

DON'T LOOK too hard, except for something agreeable. We can find all the disagreeable things in the world between our own hats and boots.

———————

DON'T DESPISE anything which you have honestly done from nature. There's a sketch, which, when I brought it home, seemed only a patch of bright green there, of violet there, and of orange here. But a year later, I chanced upon it, and found that it was an impression from nature; and that's what our sketches ought to be.

———————

PAINT WHAT you see and what you feel, if it's nothing but a cat. You can't paint a scene that you saw years ago, and of which you have only a literal drawing. If you've forgotten the poetry and the mystery, you can't get it again.

It's the way you look at a thing that makes the picture. It isn't paint, or the way in which paint is put on.

———————

PAINTING IS only an adjunct. A drawing is often better than

a painting, more apt to be kept inside of the frame. A truth which some critics never will find out

––––––––––––

YOU *can't help* doing *your own* way. You come here to be shown the way of somebody else. Where's the person that ever did anything without knowing what others had done before him? Why can we talk? Because we are talking all the time.

––––––––––––

GOING TO paint that in today? Well, then, crack ahead! *Do it!* Don't be afraid! The moment you're afraid, you might as well be in Hanover Street shopping.

––––––––––––

FIVE YEARS from today you'll say that you wish you had done what you were told to do. *Now* you all have your minds made up to what you're going to do. That's the bane of civilization.

Do as I say; and, when I see that the thing doesn't work, I'll be the first to tell you. I tell you *to paint*, because *it's going to help you* to paint, and you don't do it!

I remember your sketch of a turtle crossing over a garden walk. The most original thing that ever came out of Cambridge.

Draw. Paint. Draw. Paint. Zig-zag's the word! See a donkey go up a steep hill, and notice *how* he gets there. A kite will go straight up; But — *not unless it's held.*

If you could only see that you can paint as well as you can draw. There have been people who painted beautiful pictures, who could not draw as well as you can.

Sir Joshua Reynolds says, "I am sure that there is only one

way of painting — To begin the thing by putting it in with white and blue." If you would only handle the brush as you handle the charcoal. Go recklessly to work! You are all careful and conscientious enough. There's conscientiousness enough in this room to run fourteen water-wheels. If you were working for a man who expected you to paint four omnibuses today, six tomorrow, and eight the day after tomorrow, you'd get to working in earnest.

Do! Do! Do! Let it go, and do another!

You can't finish a thing farther than you can go. The moment you put your hand upon the canvas that part of it is finished. You never learned so much as when you painted that figure in two colours, and when you under-painted that head for me, and knew that you had only one day in which to cover the entire canvas.

It is *at last* that you'll finish. Corot doesn't finish; and he's over eighty years of age. If you all "finished" the book would be shut up.

What you do, you can do. If a person thinks by working sixteen years his work will be *better than he* is, he's mistaken.

You can do a dozen sketches while you're doing one. There are very few who can begin a picture and carry it out in the same vein. It requires peculiar skill and temperament

If you wish to prepare a work for subsequent finish, prepare it carelessly, with regard to finish. Cut it up, hew it out; and, tomorrow paint it.

You'll always run a thing down the second day. Don't get

the colour on the face the first day. Don't do it just right at first. Try to get proportions and values, flat. No delicacy, no finish. Put it in a condition that will tempt you to finish. Have it say to you, "Do it!" Why pile it up so high that it will tumble down tomorrow? Leave the top stone off, and next day you can put it on, sharp and sure.

————————

YOU ALL have ambition enough; earnestness enough. Strengthen something that you haren't got. *Get practice!*

Hand-work never did anything. If you hare a feeling or an ambition to say something you'll say it. But not today. You couldn't be born with a desire to do or say something, and not have a chance to do it

The Lord never made two leaves alike, nor two people alike.

You can't be Correggio. Neither can you be a goose. In one sense it's as hard to be an idiot as to be a Raphael. In the Conservatory, down stairs, they don't expect to play the violin in three weeks. They know that it takes years — unless you're born in a fiddle.

Snub your ideal. It costs trouble; but it's trouble that's the artist's nature. If you try to draw an eye, only as somebody else did, you'll never *do* it. Besides, when you *try* to do a thing you can't *do* it You're attempting two things at once — the *doing*, and the *trying*.

"Try!" The very word cramps you. (Drawing the figure 3 on the floor.) That's doing it. As well as I can make a 3. Now I'll try to do it. ls it as well done as the first one? No; it shows attempt and hesitation.

————————————

IN SIGNING the Declaration of Independence, John Hancock did not *try* half so hard as Stephen Hopkins. It's not quite fair, however, to mention the latter in this connection. I respect Stephen Hopkins; but I don't think he could have drawn an eye.

I must show you a drawing which Miss —— made, when she didn't know how good it was. Pupils must be kept somewhat in ignorance of their progress, and always have a step ahead. Johnny thinks he can play the fiddle *now* —— but ——!

When you have the ideal, first develop your skill, and do what your ideal suggests. Velázquez painted, and painted, and painted; and nobody cared, until he was painter at Madrid. He might have gone there as court painter with less skill than he had; but with his long practice he was ready for anything.

You have got to prepare yourselves for everything! If you only knew the trouble that is taken with horses that are to race, it would teach you a good deal. If a two-year-old colt is to run he ia not allowed to carry any weight. Tho more he develops one set of muscles the more he loses others. In the army the cavalry officers could not have walked; but they could ride five days in succession, forty or fifty miles, night and day. They couldn't make horse-shoes but they could save a whole *corps* of the army.

You need somebody to tell you at what point you require to be developed. Some one to say, "You must carry this farther." I don't say it to keep you from following your own idea.

If you would get stone out of the quarry, keep cool, use gunpowder, and let the big Irishman help you. Then clear everybody out of the way, and do your fine work. What if you had "finished" it before the blasting?

You think that you know what you want to know. I know what you want to know better than you do. I want to get you disgusted with your own ideal.

Art is cumulative. It would be easier to follow certain things in a place where you can follow them, and let the doubts come outside. Why does So-and-So go to Europe and copy a Correggio? Wouldn't I give all my old boots to see Velázquez paint for one week, one day? But I wouldn't have said that when I Was fifteen. I should have felt as you do. But suppose that I had been wise enough, had *kept my will for progress*, not for carrying out my own views; and could have been with Velázquez at sixteen years of age? I should have known how to paint. He could have told me in one week what he was ten years in learning. But every human being isn't so willing. I have never found anybody — even Millet, whom I knew well, would only talk with me. He wouldn't *show* me two things.

I've been painting thirty years. Under instruction, I could, in ten years, have learned all that I have learned — no, not all, but I could have followed any one in whom I had confidence. I went abroad to follow what I thought was the true method of painting; but I've told you more this winter, yes, sometimes more in one week, than *I* was ever told in my whole life!

Not one person in five thousand can find out anything

for himself. I've seen boys come out Couture's *atelier,* and go farther in three months than others would in three years. *They took the method at which he had arrived.* And mind that *abroad they don't tell you.* They neither show you nor tell you. Couture would say, "That's horrid! If you can't do better than that you'd better stop."

But it's always different with a man. *He has to be in earnest.* He has his living to get. If they'd shown me in Harvard College how to do mathematics, I should have been a mathematician. But I'm glad now that they didn't

You can't get too much showing. As soon as you leave your class nobody is going to be interested to show you how to do anything. Your friends will criticise and turn up their noses, but they won't show you. And while I say this, let me add it's disagreeable to put yourself in the position of a dancing-master who says, "Be graceful. Imitate me."

Look at that drawing done by one of the last year's class. Materially I can't compete with that. Among my drawings you can't find one so simply done as that. In it I recognize everything which I ever told her. I'd defy anybody to make such a drawing as that. It has all the needed elements except concentration. In it there's material enough to do better things than I ever did. I can represent a subject more closely than that; but I can't do anything so unconsciously as that is done.

Six out of twelve who are studying do a better thing than they who teach. At the same time teaching helps the teacher. I come in here and put into words the very thing that I've been trying to do in my own room. I'll be there, niggling and fooling; come in and see you doing the same thing; go back and correct myself through you. I do a thing four times as easy since I've been teaching.

You're learning a great deal, and doing very well; or I wouldn't remain in here to talk to you. To tell the truth I am more in earnest that you should get a fact than that I should. What if I had given you the instruction that I had when I was sixteen? Had made you draw with a fine point such a thing as the Apollo Belvedere, which I venture to say Phydias himself wouldn't have done. Correction is easy. But when you get the principle all wrong it's anything but easy to set you right.

Look at the pictures you thought you liked two years ago , and you can now see what is good and what is bad about them. Can see right through them.

———————————

WE STUPIDLY suppose that what is called "finish" or outside work, gives value to a thing. It is too much like the mince-pie given to a boarding-school boy at the *last* dinner of the term. It may deceive, but it doesn't mend matters.

The finish should be done in the same mood with the beginning. A highly finished imbecility is worth no more than an imbecility. Adapt your finish to the stuff that's underneath, and let it be of one piece; and don't try to make believe that you know more than you do. Don't smooth your mashed potato with a knife.

This much admired finish is like the architecture that the

countryman said was going to be put on his house by a Boston man — *after it was built!*

Oh, think of a last week's mince-pie with the added truthful date of today stamped upon its crust for a finish. This kind of thing may do in putting up mackerel and blackberries, but it won't answer in pictures!

If the truth isn't the fundamental part, there's no use in adding it as embroidery.

Tinkering isn't painting!

————————

YOU MAKE the figures 3, 4, 6, as well as you know how at first. How much better can you do if you niggle? What's the use of niggling in painting any more than in talking? What if a child can't sound R at three years of age? Let him alone. He'll come out all right. Bore him to do it and he'll be a pedant. If you know the shape of a person's nose you'll draw it If you don't you can't do it.

You say that you "want to niggle" on that face. When you're convinced that a certain thing is needed, get it by niggling *if it will* help you to do it broadly. Dot it with the point of a pen if you can do it. But when I want to make a fine line I do it with the blunt end of a stick of charcoal. You are using a large brush, and suddenly you want to make a fine line. You change brushes; and, while doing so, lose sympathy with your subject.

Somebody asked Albrecht Dürer, "What did you use in drawing that beard, that you should get such lines?" "A large brush" was the reply.

Some of you like to believe that there's another way quite as good as what I've shown you. *Don't make your exceptions until you know the rule!* You wouldn't have known the difference between this light and that dark, if I hadn't shown you. You want to feel as if this were a part of the work that don't require any brains. *You must save your brains for the most important part.* I don't say that I know how to do this; but I think I can show you in two minutes that which will save you ten years of trying. Your case is that of every one who has been educated in the ideal before they've been educated in the manipulation. I think I can show you a short way of doing certain things (unimportant), which will leave you more time in which to perfect the work of the day, to carry out your individual notions. It took you three times as long to paint that background as it ought to have taken. I would go in *not to shirk* work, but *to do it!*

I am sorry to say so much against littérateurs, but the truth is, they never had their eyes opened. They are blind. They don't know that we've got to sacrifice something to *ensemble*. They have nothing to do with the *practice* of painting. They find more art in the drawing of a landscape than in the drawing of a head, "because there are *more lines* in it." Is it lines that make the landscape? Take an opera-glass and examine the landscape painting and you may find that there isn't a line in it. They don't take into account that a tree is made with a certain amount of freedom.

The painter knows what is necessary in literature better than the *littérateur* knows what is needful in painting. Shakespeare could not paint with brushes as well as I can write a poem. A painter is necessarily a poet; but a poet is not a painter. Emerson can describe a forest in words better than I can; but I can make one in paint better than he. If he is a full man he will understand both; and if I am a full man I can understand his description as well as my own.

That's where Cambridge is short. Such knowledge counts for nothing. They forget the song that painting has sung, and listen only to Homer. A Greek professor who doesn't know what Greek Art is, isn't a Greek scholar. I don't know just what Greek was a ruler during a certain period, but I have some literary science and *ensemble*. Ignorant as I am, I know more about Homer than a Greek professor can know about Phidias. He might tell me when he was born. Well, a rat was born about that time.

People go to Europe and bring home secondhand "old masters." Get them cheap, and there's a great cry over them. But if one of those old painters were living in Boston today, not one of his works would they buy. Of their own accord they wouldn't pick up a Millet drawing or a drawing by Michelangelo. No, they go about whining, because we have "no Art in this country," and "we never shall paint like Titian." (Since Titian died there have been, in certain directions, even greater painters than he.) Such people are logs across the track!

———————————

"WON'T YOU give us an example of what you call Art

in literature?"

Well, Everett's speech at Gettysburg is what passes for "elegant literature." But Lincoln's speech was *real* literature! And *real* literature, like *real anything, is Art!*

"But why do you find so much fault with *littérateurs?*"

Because they hinder more than they help me in my work. Their notion of criticism is *fault-finding.* They are self-constituted judges of an occupation of which they are not masters. They know from what they *read,* not from what they *see.*

When their perceptions shall be keen enough to discover and encourage the first germ of w*hat has never been seen before, then only can they help us.*

I want the names of writers who have ever recognized the young Turner, Stothard, Millet, and Blake, *before they were forty.*

I would as soon listen to a *lecture* on Art as to *smell* of *music,* or to *eat the receipt of a plum pudding*!

This is the age of the tongue and the ear! We listen with hollow gaping awe to a description of the Parthenon; build our temples by contract; pay for them in greenbacks; and send to England for stamped Johnny-cake ornaments and friezes, and *pocket the difference.* We learn a *great deal* about *everything,* and *very little* about *anything!* Nothing is too thin for us. There is a market for more skim-milk than we can produce. The cream sours, and is given to the cat!

Keep up the practice of the eye and the hand. For it will be needed later.

Our literature helps Art as an Academy helps an orchard.

Spring hangs a rose on every tree, the graft and the thorn alike. Nature's pruners, wind, hail-storm, and cankerworm, save half the fruit that nature cannot ripen.

Then comes the scholar, with stick and stone, flail, pillow-case, and front tooth, absorbs and decides upon the rest. If there's one seed of the whole year left to grow black enough to sprout, it is sheltered in some hidden "frozen thaw."

I'm glad of it. It all helps. Nothing creates such thirst in us as the pursuit of knowledge. It has been so ever since the time of Adam. And there's *some* juice in all fruit!

Nothing takes the taste of grammar out of a boy's mouth like a green apple. Every school should have its *orchard*, as every army its schooner-load of onions and lemons, to stave off mould and scurry.

Yet, as I say, *it all helps.* But it don't help—the—*apple!*

ART BELONGS to this age just as the air belongs to it. "Classic!" Who would have said, two thousand years ago, that Millet and Delacroix would be classic? Give me the fellow that can find some honey in the flower that grows. Talk about Hymettus. We have just as good material to make painters of as we have to make poets. The poets have had the libraries of the world to read, while the painters have had to expatriate themselves. Instead of taking down a dictionary they've had to take a steamer and go to Europe.

These *littérateurs* would keep us back a century. They bully the public. A city goes to see a collection of paintings, and likes them. A swell comes in. "*This* is all wrong. But *here* is something that is good. *This* was done four hundred and fifty years before Christ."

Somebody may come to Boston today and paint fine things; and there must be somebody to recognise that they are fine; come forward and encourage; and not get in the way and snub.

Instead of fault-finding and criticizing, the literary man should say, "What can I do to help you? I have fine pictures (and money, perhaps). How can I assist you?" Does he or any such man say so? No; they think more highly of themselves than of art They wouldn't have lent a hand in the time of Phidias any more than in the time of Ben Butler!

Don't hurry — or you'll never get through!

Decide what, you're going to jdo, and do it in three minutes. This dilly-dallying makes me think of a schoolboy trying to bound Massachusetts. "It's bounded by— by — by — (another boy prompts — 'Rocky Mountains') Oh, yes, by the Rocky Mountains!"

Don't do any fiddling which keeps you from thinking. If you want variety change your aim, but don't use less powder. Change your aim, but not your force. Decide what you're going to have. When you have decided, turn off the difference between face, coat, and background. The way you do is to think you won't put this in quite so dark, or it will look like a negro, etc. In a word, you get up a million reasons which have nothing to do with the thing but to retard progress. Have it dark at first. Let it be so; and when you go on it won't look too dark.

We worry ourselves too much about the doing of a thing because we've arrived at a mental stopping-place before we've begun our work.

"But what if we know nothing?"

It would be a great deal better for you. We'll reverse wheels. Would that suit you any better? Let me say the opposite, and you would find ground to oppose me. *Painting is the hardest thing in the world,* and I must arrange certain things on certain platforms so that you may know somewhat how to go on. It's impossible to make a picture without "values." Values are the basis. If they are not, tell me what is the basis. Show me the pictures in the world that have not values for their first fact. They furnish the only way in which anything is visible — the only way in which a thing can be represented.

"But can't you get the same effect by interior modelling?"

You can get nothing flat. Albrecht Dürer, with an outline, knew how to make an outline look like a firm, full figure. He began with firmness, and fullness, and finished with delicacy. You can't make an eye by making an eyelash. However Albrecht Dürer began, his things have an *ensemble*. But he didn't get it in a day. Hercules may have strangled a serpent when he was a baby, but there was a time when he couldn't.

"Dürer worked in his own way?"

No, nor did anybody else at first. They all worked in the manner of some one else, in the way they were shown. Raphael after Perugino, Vandyke after Rubens. If Albrecht Dürer had lived in Venice he would have been a Venetian painter. As it was he worked as the old German artists had worked; and we cannot but feel that when he came to see the Venetians, he wished that he could have seen them earlier and modified his work by their influence.

But talking is the least useful thing in painting. I have my ideas, but I hate to force them upon anybody. I am right, just as far as I know. The less that's said about it the better, and the more work will be done. Instead of trying to get what I do believe, you say, "but" and "if" and we might talk all day to no use.

———————

FOR YEARS, Millet painted beautiful things, and nobody looked at them. They fascinated me, and I would go to Barbizon and spend all the money I could get in buying his pictures. I brought them to Boston. "What is that horrid thing?" "Oh, it's a sketch by a friend of mine." Now he is the greatest painter in Europe.

———————

KEEP THE head all together. Don't try to finish one part. That's the fun of painting— to keep the whole thing. People who always offer an "if" or a "but" would say, "Ah, but what if you hare a canvas fifty feet long?" I say, treat it as you would a small piece of paper. Run away the oftener from your work, and keep up an intense interest in it. That's the difficulty about portrait-painting. To give the drapery character and fitness, and keep it subservient to the head. Your idiot says, "Just look at the painting of that velvet!" Ay, but where's the head and the figure? An ape can paint velvety but he can't keep it where it belongs with reference to the head.

I remember that Homer speaks of the "broad-girdled nurse." I thought, as a boy, how well that described her. I didn't care whether her girdle was trimmed with beads or not.

I often hear that I paint drapery "carelessly." But there are four or five different kinds of carelessness. I am striving hard to get what people call *careless*, but which I call *nature*. To me nature doesn't look prigged up. I could more easily paint neatness than this ease and grace which I try to represent in my so-called "carelessness."

LOOK AT the boy. Don't look at his nostrils. That little hole is where the nostril *isn't*. You look so hard for a nostril that you've given him a nostril and a half. You seem to say "What is it that the Lord didn't intend me to see? Oh, I have it. The nostril!" You make me think of the Irishman who said that "somebody bad stolen his keyhole!" The hollow is there, and the surroundings pen it in. See, I make a hollow with my hand, and you try to draw it. Will you draw simply a hole, or will you draw a hand with a hollow through it?

LOOK AT IT, and decide what kind of a line it is; and then, without looking again, draw the line firmly. Sixteen little lines guessed at don't do it.

———————

WHEN YOU intend to paint a white man, don't make his face as black as a negro's. Needn't be a Darwinian in painting! Get to your journey's end the first day if you can. If not, go on tomorrow.

———————

REAL FINISH must be of the same quality as real beginning.

———————

THE NEEDLE only points *towards* the North. It does not *go* there. If you undertake to *go* there you freeze to death.

———————

I TOLD YOU to paint the light on that cheek, with a single stroke of the brush. In your work I see two or three, as if you had niggled and patted in an undecided way.

"I put it on with one stroke, but it was a little too dark."

No matter; take that for your key-note and go on. Your picture would simply hare been a little lower in tone, but what of that? You spread your fingers over the keys of a piano and strike a chord. If too high or too low, you need not try again, but play on in that key. So in painting. Remembering that it is easier to transpose in painting than in music.

Yes, let it stay. Don't correct your little faults. Why, you correct this and that, and that, and first you know you have nothing but a dish of hash!

———————

SUSTAIN YOUR form by making distinct outlines — of cobalt and light-red, which you can make dark or light, as you please.

You can paint them out if you like; but put them in, if they all have to come out again.

———————

WE MAY *study* the works of the *classic* artists, but we cannot imitate them. We must, each of us, sing his own song. like Henri Regnault, we may admire Michelangelo, as first and greatest; and like him feel that we cannot tell our story in *his* way.

———————

WITH A GOOD eye for colour goes an eye for the niceties of drawing.

———————

PAINT THAT little girl's face as you would a tea-rose.

———————

THERE'S NOTHING like calling a *sketch* "done" before it *is* done!

———————

YOU DON'T have to be literal to a line to make an impression. Moonlight pictures are apt to look as if you had dipped the thing in ink, and half washed it out. A sketch should look *one thing* instead of sixteen.

———————

ART IS ABOUT the only occupation in which people can do what, they please without consulting their neighbours.

———————

THE PASSAGE from the eyebrow to the hair is beautiful. See how the hair of the brow turns towards the hair of the head, as if there were a mutual attraction! Then, look at the counter-curves which the lines of the hair make as they come upon the flesh. The forehead, or front, has its curtain of hair. So has the temple, and the cheek. It is so with every head in the room.

You may *know* all this, and represent it; but if you don't *feel* it, you'll never succeed in painting it. This *feeling* is what makes the difference between a wooden thing and a beautiful fascinating picture.

———————

YOUR FLOWERS are well done. Really amusing! So much like nature. But I wish you would dispense with these black backgrounds. You like them because they disengage so easily, but you lose a chance for gradations which would make your flowers not only decorative, but a picture besides. These black grounds tempt you because everything looks well on them. Just as any colour looks well on a negro woman, while one with a peachy complexion finds that there are colours which don't improve her looks.

———————

SO THEY SAY that the portrait of Mr. ——— is not like him. I'd like to know how much a portrait by Titian would look like nature. We need some such portraits here to show people how near the greatest artists have come to representing the *exactness* of life.

———————

DON'T FOOL with transparent colours. Not at first, certainly. Stop using bitumen to begin with. If you want it, use it later; but don't begin with it. I've used too much transparent colour. Always do, always did, and always hope I shan't. Real "transparency" is the quiet relief of an eye in shadow, against a forehead and cheek in light.

———————

THE BIBLE is full of practical sayings. Only the workers can fully understand it. To the rest of the world it is all a kind of sentiment; but to the worker it is earnest and practical. Look at what it says about *fasting*. Don't the worker know that it is all true? You can't work after a heavy dinner of pork!

———————

SOME PEOPLE say that "The Age of Painting is past, The Age of Sculpture is past" etc., as if painting and sculpture might not belong to all time. We shall not see another era of Greek Sculpture. Probably not an era of painting just like what has been. But *there are possibilities in the future!*

What is called the Age of Painting was a great wave which came and disappeared. But there may be others almost as great, although different.

The truth is, there are so many people looking back into the past that they would not see great things that might happen today. If Homer were to come here and sing, they would say, "Hold on! You're in our way. *We're looking back into the Past!*"

Literature never began to comprehend what painting is. Literature is ahead. Music is coming up. Painting will come along afterwards. We're babies yet; but we still live. We're not stuffed; and we're crawling along.

The general principles of music and of sculpture are easier to talk about than the general principles of painting. Look at what a critic says of some noodles. "At any rate they have this in common with the old masters — persistent labour." *So has a jackass!*

Today, people take it for granted that they *know painting;* but they have so much sympathy with music that they are really afraid that they don't know much about that. Having learned Yankee Doodle they push on for something ahead of it. Well, it's a beautiful ambition —to want to know the best.

(Models — Mother and Child.) NOTHING COULD be more beautiful! Yet we come in and say, "That profile isn't elegant," etc. We shut our eyes to what *is* there, while we complain of what *isn't*.

No neck, no waist, but great breadth. That shows the baby. Reduce this to simple elements; then put in just enough to show what these things are. Look to see what is beautiful there, and you can put up with a good deal of bawling!

WHY MAKE fifty thousand chances at that figure when you can do it all in one? The line of that sofa is straight and horizontal. Take the trouble to hold up your brush horizontally, and compare it with the lines of what you want to draw. You can't make me believe that the sofa has been wobbling around all the morning, just to suit your perspective.

Remember that you are not painting pictures. You are

learning to paint .

You are eternally fussing about little things. Try, for once, not to be afraid of plenty of colour and of good large brushes. Go and buy some paints. Get some dark, and some light paints. Put them on your palette. Go to work largely, and you'll paint first-rate.

———————

You ought to get impressions of nature whenever you walk or drive. Get half-a-dozen, and come in and paint them, all in one day.

———————

(*Millet's "Sheep Shearer."*) — See the firmness of neck and shoulder, and how you feel the flatness of the back; and the roundness of the arm? Why don't people see these things? Because they begin by criticizing, instead of absorbing. They say, "What's that hard outline?" Millet had painted fifty years, and yet he dug on that picture ten days after I thought it was done. It's a wonder! There are no pictures finer. As fine things in that as in Michelangelo. Don't you feel the whole thing? That's *"painting!"*

———————

One hundbed years from now, Turner will be counted among the greatest men who have ever lived. His colour is wonderful! He could carry the scale higher and farther than any one else. Could get dark without using black, or brown even. His colour is iridescent. The Venetians could get such colour only by painting transparently. But Turner is solid, clear, throughout.

———————

I BELIEVE that the best paintings of landscape are made from memory. Of course you must study nature carefully for certain details, but for the *picture*, paint it in-doors, from memory. I never saw Millet out with an umbrella. When before nature you are so much occupied with representing what you see, that you can't study combination and composition. You can't make a *picture!*

———————

You MAKE CAREFUL and excellent outlines already, so you had better draw objects for light and shade. This will help *you* more than drawing simple form. With leather, bread, and charcoal, you can make a picture, without a line in it. That's the peculiar pill that you need to take. Try to see *with how little* you can make a picture. You'll put the *muchness* in, because you are very careful of outline.

Rub your paper all over black. Have *one* light, and a general gray tint, with the dark dark enough.

See what makes the *picture*. not what makes the *thing*. It's the impression of the thing that you want to get. See how near you can realize the *impression* of certain things. The effect of a drawing done in a finical way is to make the observer rub his nose against it, and say, "Oh, there's a light in a fly's eye!" You want to make people receive the same impression that you have received from nature. Then you can make things beautiful and exact, so long as they don't interfere with the impression. Do things from memory, because in that way you remember only the *picture*. No matter what you do, but make the thing look like a picture.

WE ARE ALL cursed by the nonsense of our early teachers. I took lessons, like the rest of you, with a pointed lead pencil and a measure; and today I feel the restraint which that way of beginning imposed upon me — so strong is the impression made by early lessons. We have all been taught by people who never did anything, never loved anything in the way of art. How can such people teach?

Do *fascinating* things. Not smart ones. Nobody ever tucks a *smart* sketch under his arm and runs home with it. Paint your own Impressions. Tom and Dick won't like the result; but, by and by, along comes Harry, who says, "By Jove, I've seen that very thing in nature!"

DO AS I say, not as I do! I come in here and tell you these things not only to help *you*, but to strengthen *myself* for my *own* work.

"HOW SHALL I finish my owl?" You've got his *eye*. Now you'd better put his *body* around it !

WHY MAKE that drawing look like a cobweb, trimmed with feathers ?

"I want it to look *soft*."

Softness isn't the only beauty. A good deal of soap is soft
Bad fruit is *too soft!* Remember, that a child's cheek, if it is
soft, is also *firm!*

DRAWING SHOULD be considered not an accomplishment,
but a necessity. Any one who can make the letter D can learn
to draw. Learning to draw is learning the grammar of a language. Anybody can learn the grammar, but whether you have
anything to say, that is another thing.

There is scarcely a child whose first impulse is not to scribble
on the wall or any fresh piece of paper. It is almost the first
thing that he wishes to do, and there is hardly a parent who
does not cuff him for it.

The child's scribbling on the margin of his school-books is
really worth more to him than all he gets out of them. To him
the margin is the best part of all books, and he finds in it the
soothing influence of a clear sky in a landscape.

IF ANY ONE doubts what a flat tint will do, let him see
the shadow of a rabbit on the wall, which he can make with
his own hands.

YOU SOFTEN the fibre of your memory by fastening yourself
too closely to your work and your model. You *could* come here
and look at that figure, and go away and draw it, if you had
accustomed yourself to work in that way. Some niceties of
nature you must correct and refine from life; but you can get

values, proportion, etc., by observation and memory.

Some of the most vivid renderings of nature have been done after nature had passed. How else can you paint a thunder-shower, a sunset, a flying cloud, a galloping horse? You don't trust yourself enough. You are too timid. If you were to have that head only four minutes you would put in something that would be like it; but, if you are to have it all day, you twist it all out of shape. Corot says, when he was in Rome he tried to draw groups; but they would move before he got one nose drawn. So he decided what the general form would be, and how one figure corresponded with another.

———————

PICTURES ARE never *simple* enough! An intelligent old friend of mine tells me, with a wink of his eye, that he os "looking for a picture with nothing in it!" He says that Allston's painting of "Elijah and the Raven" hasn't much in it; but *he* is looking for something with less. We all put in *too much*, but *not enough!*

———————

Don't keep so near your work. It looks very well to you as you sit there, but to me, coming into the room, I see a want of gradation in your background, and a lack of strength in your shadows. Your work is earnest, but you must make three persons of yourself. One to go on, one to be careful, one to criticise. When you go away from your work you become your own critic.

As soon as we get so that we can handle our own work in

that way, we become giants!

We want the Best. But we never fearlessly criticise each other. There is always, some sensitiveness.

———————

Your WORK IS earnest, and *you* may be a little careless for a while. Get the geography of your masses at first. Put in a flat, broad, distinct shadow for the darks. In your endeavour to get the mystery of that shadow you fail to give its form and strength. You don't have to draw an object if you draw the shape of the shadows.

Don't be afraid of spoiling your drawing. You draw to learn.

———————

Your BOY IS a pathetic little chap. An outsider would not see what my experience shows me — that, in your timid, delicate drawing, only half expressed, there is appreciation of the character of the little fellow. I like that timidity and delicacy. It will serve you later. *Now* you must look for *strength*. Intensify your shades. Don't let the sentiment so captivate you that you lose the geography. In your aspiration you shut your eyes to the rocks on which you may founder. Throw out your plummet and see where you are.

Yours is too round.

"I thought it looked round."

Yes, roundness is a *fact*. His cap is round; shoulders round; he stoops, and his back is round. Therefore, seek for an opposite, and find all the *straight lines* and *sharp angles*. In that way you vitalize your work !

Look for the round, but *look for the square contained in that round.* Chop it out with an axe; and sand-paper it afterwards.

I want to see you work as hard to *draw* as I do to *find fault,* and you'll do tip-top things!

The critics make holes in us, as the Brazilian bores holes into his silver porcupine, and sells it to be decorated with toothpicks.

Nature, with *her* quill, protects even a *goose!*

An artist wants neither flattery nor ignorant abuse. There's no excuse for a criticism being worse than the work criticized. With all that's said about "carelessness" we ask the critic to put as much care and thoughtfulness into *his* work as the painter puts into *his!*

How often a little coating of quicksilver on the spectacles interferes with our perceptions of others' works.

Art at any rate means something accomplished! In almost everything else there is too much "talky, talky." But here. I am, doing just that I decry.

There is a great deal of talk about "conscientious work" in painting. As well talk to the bird about conscientiousness in his singing! Conscientiousness and justice are stations which have been reached and passed before any fine work appears. They are almost material limits compared with the overflow that Art is. They serve the purpose of the trader, but not of the artist who cannot *stop* to do conscientious work. He *begins* far ahead of that. If painters stopped at conscientiousness they would cheat the world out of half they have done. Imagine Paganini playing "conscientiously!"

DRAWING THAT ginger jar? Well, how do you get on?

"I can't get it round enough"

Not round enough? You've made it *too round*. You have tried so hard for the quality of roundness that you have sacrificed everything else. You have forgotten to keep the brilliancy, the colour, and the appearance of porcelain. You should have tried to make it look sonorous, hard. Not like a plum-pudding, or any other kind of a pudding.

Take the *whole* thing, and look for its character. You say it is round; but is it round like a billiard ball? No, it has *flat* planes. Look at the flat, angular shape of its "high light." See how its shadows are great flat planes. If you go on working thoughtlessly, without thinking seriously how that jar really appears, you'll make it rounder and rounder every day.

Things declare themselves flat. Bad drawings look like grapes. Every little round represented.

Do the character first. You'll get it in the first four lines, if you get it at all. The character, the *character*, the CHARACTER! That's the beauty, the *beauty*, the BEAUTY!

Keep this in mind, that it is the definite, individual character of an object which makes beauty. The effect of light is what makes things beautiful. Light never stops to find beauty! Half of the beautiful pictures in the world are painted from people who are not beautiful.

Take a figure on a teapot. If you were to see the woman from whom it is painted, you would say, "Oh, isn't she *horrid! I never saw such a fright!*" But the artist saw something that he liked in this "fright," and painted what he saw, and, looking at the teapot, you say, "Oh, what a lovely figure. Where *did* the artist find such a beautiful creature?"

The truth is, that *The painter does not deny what the Lord has made!*

Think of those hideous dwarfs that Velázquez painted. You would turn away from them if you were to meet them. But *he gave the character!* Therefore, his pictures are beautiful

In Art you can't do as you do in nature. You are trying to represent, with *charcoal*, a *porcelain* jar. You must *represent*, not *imitate!* Not easy to do this. Look to see where your light comes. Look to see where your shadow comes. Cut it up into planes. Look to *extend* your lights; not to diminish them. Look sharp for concaves. Not too much for convex lines.

You sit too near your work. You see only the *handiwork*. If you were to look at it from a distance you would see the *quality*.

Look for *effect*, not handiwork. You can't do that jar as it *is*. Do it as it *seems*. Make your drawing "carry" across the room. Make it so strong that when you enter the door you cannot, at first, tell which is the drawing and which is the jar.

IF A MAN is going to do anything, the sooner he begins to believe that he knows nothing, the better. Talk to business men about business, and see what they'll think of you!

IT DON'T improve a kettle to make it blacker than it is. Everybody has an idea that a kettle is black, but perhaps it isn't half so black as we think it is.

Things made to look exactly "like" would be so hideous that you couldn't sit in the room with them.

SPREAD THE *light* on broadly as sunshine, but handle the passage from light into shadow as delicately as you would strew flowers upon a child's grave.

"WHY DIDN'T you like Cambridge?"

Because I love Art!

Cambridge was like Kaulbach's pictures. It was all literature. There was nothing there to stimulate or develop the perceptions, and everything to suppress instinct and enthusiasm. One learned neither to see nor to feel. Everything was a *task*, a parrot's training.

I don't care to know what somebody says *has* been done. I want to *see what has been done,* and I want to *see something done.* I want *to do.* I want to *learn to do!*

I don't want to write a theme on subjects of which I know nothing, in order to practice my ignorance. I don't want my intelligence to be gauged by *marks*, or my rank to depend upon another's failure.

I don't care to learn to do exactly as everybody else does. One absorbs commonplace enough without being instructed.

I like Joy in my studies, and I don't like *literary indigestions!*

But that was thirty years ago; and I suppose it is all different now!

———

I was sketching the other day near a foundry, and one person after another stopped and commented. Some passed on, considerately leaving me to attend to my work, without asking questions. An Irishman queried, "What are you doing that for?"

"I paint to learn" was my reply.

"Strange way to *learn* anything. I'd rather *pound iron!*" And he was right.

Of course the critic came along; one of those people that know everything.

"You haven't got chimneys enough on that house. You've got only three, and there are four."

I could but reply, "The only way is, to *do it yourself!*"

———

"Have you been in California? They say that we should see the wonders of the Yosemite Valley if we wish to look at scenery."

The extraordinary does not come within the province of Art. You can't represent the height of the Alps or the Sierras.

We must keep ourselves within the limits of possibility.

As soon as travelling becomes easy, people spend their time in reading the Boston Herald.

DON'T MAKE your drawings *easy to understand*. No matter if people don't understand them. Leave something for the imagination to supply.

SHOULD ONE speck of Art appear here it would be made into mincemeat in a trice by those whose power of destroying is superior to their power of creating. Some of our critics are like unskillful gardeners weeding carrot-beds. They seem to pull up all the *carrots*.

WE LAUGH to think that Newton's *dog* did not see the apple fall! We forget that few of us are Newtons; and, that had *we* been of the party, we should have had to share honours with Bow-wow.

PAINTERS CAN'T create circumstances and do the work at the same time, any more than you can push a boat by blowing the bellows, or a soldier make a cause and fight a battle, and pay himself his stipend all at once.

Velázquez never laid up any money for himself.

"HOW CAN I improve this eye?"

Move it from the cheek-bone to its socket in the skull!

THE MOST expressive phrases of this year's coinage: CHROMO CIVILIZATION, and GREEDY BARBARISM!

————————

PAINTING IS looked at as an accomplishment. But it is the *only universal language.*

All nature is creation's picture-book. Painting only can *describe* everything which can be seen, and suggest every emotion which can be felt.

Art reaches back into the babyhood of time, and is man's only lasting monument.

————————

SPEAKING OF GREEK Art, Lessing says, "Beautiful statues, fashioned from beautiful beings, reacted upon their creators; and the state was indebted, for its beautiful men, to beautiful statues. With us the susceptible imagination of the mother seems to express itself only in monsters."

————————

THERE WAS A law against caricature among the Thebans, commanding the artist to make his pictures more beautiful than the originals; and condemning the unworthy artifice of obtaining a likeness by exaggerating the deformities of the model.

————————

"NOTHING IS easier than to express extremes."

————————

READ TAINE. Read Blake. Read William Hazlitt. Read Browning.

————————

OUR IDEA of "finish" is that everything should be smooth. Our arms should be carved upon pumice-stone; field — sand-paper; and crest — a *file rampant!*

A bird is finished when he can fly.

Ruskin calls finish "an added truth." I wish him joy and a long life! He confounds it with death and the judgment-day!

Finish is *leaving off anywhere an the outside, after having filled the interior.* Stopping before you or others are tired out. Before you are a corpse, or before you have killed your work. I mean that this is the receipt for us poor weak ones. Michelangelo, and the diamond, seem *finished* without difficulty, because the *substance is finished!*

Stop with some breath in your body. Even with your work *ahead of you.* Not as though you had hauled it along to die of starvation on the milestone *beyond the last!*

Most work is *deliberately murdered*, in the hope that it may never speak of its author's *incapacity.*

Don't try to put much of Michelangelo's finish on your work. Don't try to put a hard polish upon soft stuff. Swap jack-knives. But don't lose time in adding a "truth" that won't stay there !

Most so-called "highly finished" work is hidebound, and has that look of goneness, that unmistakably empty look which a house presents when the family have moved into the country. Rotten-stone on the door-knob foils to deceive.

You have finished *the skin* only. Please don't *begin* where Nature *leaves off.* To put the yolk in after the shell is finished is never a neat job!

You can't *add* or subtract a "truth." A truth is complete, and to be let alone. Adding a truth is like polishing a soap-bubble. You can't amalgamate truths. All the truths in the world won't finish an argument or a picture.

Trying to add "truths" has nearly ruined English Art!

When English Artists paint their *impressions*, their Art has weight. When they accumulate *facts*, their pictures are like dictionaries.

John Ruskin's receipts make a book, but never made a painter, and never can make a *picture*.

Scientific scrutiny may take things to pieces, but it can't put them together again.

It dissolves diamonds, and obtains ——gas!

It takes a painter to make a painter. It takes a painter to make a picture. It takes a painter to appreciate a picture.

———

VERY FEW poets get their inspiration from nature. The majority of them hare read other poets, and they use the same ideas, clothed in different language. The painter has to go directly to nature, or he is a mere copyist. He cannot paint his picture like somebody else. He must tell his own story, if he has any to tell. Please to look out of the window. You'll get something different from what you get out of books, for it never has been seen before!

———

BEAUTY IS that little something which fills the whole world, and is neither contained in a straight nose, a long eyelash, nor a blue mountain. Some see it in a leg of mutton; others in a compound fracture; and to expect others to accept one's own definition of it is as absurd as to expect all humanity to use the same toilet-brush.

Don't poke the fire until you have some coal ready to put on. It's too much like criticism. It kills instead of helping.

If we only would dare to say what we believe I — what we like. We pick a little flower in the field, and look at it by ourselves, certain that no one sees us. At last somebody comes along. "Hulloa, then *you* like a potato-blossom! So do I. But I never dared to say so."

If you don't have fun in your studies you'll get nothing but pedantry for a result

---

Try not to see as much as you see!

The height which the balloon and the pedant reach depends on how much lighter their filling is than the air which sustains life.

If you want stuffing go to a pedant; but for development listen to a bird. The one of all joy makes a solitude. The other of solitude makes a song.

ART TEACHES you the philosophy of life, and if you can't learn it from art, you can't learn it at all. It shows you that there is no *perfection*. There is light and there is also shadow. Everything is in half-tint.

A MAN IS nothing except in his relation to others of the human race. We are all too selfish, not ready enough to give. And yet *giving* is *receiving*.

You are getting too anxious over your work. You are losing the idea of the whole, and troubling yourself too much about the half-tints and the grays, things that the Lord never thought of. There is conscientiousness all through your studies. A little more tranquillity, a little more simplicity, would carry your work along immensely. If you bad a good idiot to work for you, you would make great strides. You cut your things all into hash. Make, for once, a good solid piece of roast beef. Extend your lights. If you get your work all puckers, sweep them right out. You feel as if you had been studying too many years, and as if you ought to hare arrived somewhere by this time. In your haste to get there as soon as somebody else, you undertake to canter right in. The fact is, you are already *there*; and, indeed, getting beyond. You are too far out, too much in advance, — like an army stretched out too thin. You must draw in a little, work quietly and not Worry.

You all undertake to judge too much of your own work. Why, it's none of your business this judging. You are over conscientious. You are already in heaven. Don't get uneasy and wriggle about, or you may find yourselves in hot water. You can afford to sit still just where you are. Poor child, you don't believe it. I'm afraid you will have to lead a worrying life.

No, you must not ask yourselves if you are improving: that is my business. I will indicate the direction in which you ought to go, and if you can show me any better I am willing. Don't crucify yourselves, don't saw yourselves in two; go right along; have faith in the direction in which I send you, and believe that time is going to help you to what you want

Draw that ear carefully: it is permanent; always staying just in its place. It has no change of expression, like the other features, which, in a sketch, you are permitted to draw with a little less care, because you may reach an expression without great painstaking. You have the *ensemble* of that head, but the ear shows that you don't know how to draw, — shows just how long you have been studying. At the same time there are plenty of people who could draw that ear with correctness, but who would have no idea of producing the *ensemble* as you have done.

And here I must repeat what I have said so often. Trace Albrecht Dürer, see how he renders an ear. Some of you are tracing, but not all. When you come here in the morning and find that you don't feel just like work, take out the Dürer photographs, trace, copy, do them from memory, make them a part of yourself.

You all work too much from life. You have a model every,

morning, but it does not follow that you are going to be inspired just because it is eleven o'clock. Some day, when you don't feel like painting from nature, take still life. There is no anxiety about that. You are getting ahead of yourselves, of your power of doing, — like the man who took me to drive with a horse that needed constant urging. We were tugging along with a good deal of effort, when he exclaimed, "Well, I'll never again try to sell this horse!"

"Is this his usual gait?" I asked.

"I am sorry to say that it is. It seems sometimes as if I must jump over his head in my desire to get there before he does."

You don't drill enough. None of you know what mechanical drawing is. Go into the schools where that and nothing else is taught, and try to add their exactness to what you are doing now.

As you can't draw an ear, suppose that you try that especially. Look at any fine ear in the room; never was any flower so beautiful. Look at the back of the ear how it is joined to the head, and see the splendid curve that it makes. Why, it's like Greek art. Look at the front of the ear, how it belongs to the face. It follows the gesture of the nose, and also the line of jaw. When a laugh comes, how this line seems to carry the ear higher, till you could fancy it ending in a point, like the ear of a fawn.

And the colour of the ear, rosy and pearly. I don't think I should have known how beautifully an ear could be painted if I had not seen Couture do it. Such ears as he could paint! They'd make you howl.

You want the colour of a Rubens in an ear. And, by the way, Rubens is not half enough considered. A great painter, — great for his swing, his gesture, his way. Stop at Burrage's window some morning, and see that woodcut done by Rubens's own hand. Look at the distance, the air in it; see how one thing helps another. Rubens's glory is in his grandeur, largeness, breadth, air. Look at that picture and see how it dwarfs everything about it. Why, the modem engravings look like the little pictures you see in Paris made of human hair, — look like twaddle by the side of that Rubens. Ruskin would probably find fault with the foliage; but his trees look like trees. Study that picture and see what song he sings.

"When I saw his pictures abroad, I knew them at once because they were always the ones that seemed to me to be springing from their frames; and I remember that I always liked his portraits."

His portraits are magnificent. Rubens's pictures are what we need to see to keep us up to the colour there is in nature. Yet, look at him, the diplomat, the swell, sitting down with a fine pen to copy and trace an etching by Da Vinci. He couldn't do it, but he wanted to; and he tried.

How we all want to do a thing like somebody else. Don't you believe that, when Albrecht Dürer went to Italy, he wished he had gone before, instead of shutting himself up in that little town in Germany, but he has done, in his way, just as beautiful things as anybody.

———————

"Is THAT sketch of Miss B. like her?"

No matter if it is or isn't. To do it is the first thing. Have it like is the second. The figure is *elegant*, — which is something that most people think nothing of, so much are they taken up with likeness. Then it is *naive!* The head goes into the background in such an unconscious way. It is skillfully painted, and I know that you could not have done it two years ago.

"Then you think we do go on, even when we feel that we are not gaining as we ought to?"

You can't help going on; but you can't always see the steps. Nothing is hard if you take the right steps to do it. Of a sudden we find out that our teachers are great noodles; and in our despair at finding that we are so far behind where we ought to be, we try to jump over the river at one bound. You must throw in one stone at a time, and by and by you will see one floating on the top. — "Oh, but there's Susan Jane going on alone." — Never mind; she has to come to the mud too, and then she must begin to throw in her stones and build her foundation. The people who have got the thing called "success," have reached it without knowing it

————————

You MUST know, before you start a drawing, just where your figure is going to come upon the canvas. See how Michelangelo planned every comer of his work. Most of us put a little bit of a figure in the middle of a large background that is of no use. Look at the Greek coins: no waste space, every part filled. Then look at our cent, with the figure so small that it looks like a crow in a wilderness.

DON'T DWELL too much on what you *have* done. Go on, and don't paint each sketch as if it were to be the last thing you were to do in life. Believe that you are going to make hundreds of them, and go on to the next.

YOU MUST feel that there is a head under that hat. I Draw a line through the hat where you know that the top of the head ought to come, and see how the hat looks then. Ostrich feathers won't take the place of brains.

WHEN ANYTHING profiles you must have it profile to mean something.

PEOPLE ARE apt to think that painting is simply skillful work.

WILL IT to be flat, and it will come so. Look at the work of the Japanese. They *knew* the thing, and then put it down. No high light in their decorations: fiat tints, with due regard to values.

BE CONTENTED to do something in the direction in which the thing *is*, not in the way you *feel* it. Build up your power of doing actualities. Be convinced that you can't help putting in some of your own feeling and originality. Don't run around trying to be original, standing on your head or diving under water. Believe that if you work and let yourself go, all will come out right. If you work only for what you feel, and not for reality, you work all the time with one oar.

Don't be afraid of spoiling your work. You can't spoil anything in this world. There's a great deal of work to be done for the sake of learning how it is done. I've seen John Millet sit down in Millet's studio, and, without a word of encouragement, work three weeks from a plaster cast.

"But when we cany our tilings home —"

Tour parents don't like them? Of course they don't, they haven't been through enough. Make a drawing equal to Michelangelo, and there isn't a parent in this city that is going to know how good it is. They go to the Louvre and admire a drawing with Michelangelo's name under it; but take away that name and put on another and they won't look at the drawing.

Don't mind what your friends say of your work. In the first place they all think you're an idiot; in the next place, they expect great things of you; in the third place, they wouldn't know if you did a good thing. Until we come to study art we are not aware of the ignorance there is about it.

Artists have to create their audiences. They have to do their own work and educate the public at the same time. Nobody cared for Corot's pictures at first. He had to teach people how to like them. The same with Raphael. His pictures were not understood; but he went on painting, and in time he was appreciated.

———————

GET THE general form, lightly; next, the shadows, loosely, — not too much indicated. Having blocked it out, begin to define forms, giving those lines which are most characteristic. Don't keep up this white-washing process of pat, patting, or your work will grow softy, softy.

———————

"I'M AFRAID of losing my drawing!"

Lose it, lose it? Why, you seem to think that your drawing is *good*, you are so anxious to keep it. Throw it away! Drawing is not one of the "lost arts." If you do lose it, you can find it.

———————

YOUR ARE all too intelligent to draw. You seem to say, "This model has black hair. Black, black, black," and you get it nothing but black. Why, the light on a stove-pipe is whiter than the shadow on a white shirt. You all *know* too much to draw. Everything that you know you put down in black lines. You know that she has a line between her lips, and you make a note of it with charoal; and as charcoal is black, all your notes are black.

———————

Is THAT all the charcoal you have? You seem to be trying to "make it go round," — like boarding-school butter.

———————

YOU MUST set yourselves ahead by studying fine things. If you don't you never will do them. I've told you over and over again whose works to draw, — Michelangelo, Raphael, Albrecht Dürer, Hans Holbein, Mantegna. Get hold of something of theirs; hang it up in your room; trace it, copy it, draw it from memory over and over, until you *own* it, as you own "Casabianca," and "Mary had a little lamb." You can't draw an eye well until you know how some great master has drawn it. That's why, in Europe, they would make you draw three years from the antique before they would allow you to touch a brush.

But I want you to get more fun out of your work, so I let you go ahead by first studying "masses." Now, as you are strong on masses, don't keep eternally working on what is your strong point. Find out where your work is weak, and strengthen that. If you were going to raise a plain, would you cover it with little piles of earth, or would you put it all in one pile, and by and by let it topple over?

"But what if we are in the bottomless pit and can't see our way out of it?"

You'll have so large a number of people with you that you won't be lonely, and can have a jolly good time. Besides, being at the bottom you can get no farther *down*, and will soon begin to go up. And it's going on and up that's the fun of studying, not the arriving at a place. Arriving is the end. What does Browning say? —

"If success were intended,
Why, heaven would begin ere earth ended."

"What is the chief trouble with *my* drawing?"

The same as with the others. You don't know anything about fine things. You don't draw that mouth because you have never traced or copied a mouth that is well-drawn.

"Isn't it bad because. I tried too hard to make it look just like the model?"

No ; it is bad because you don't know how to draw it; and the reason you don't know how to draw it is because you haven't studied the way in which a master would do it. There are good things in your sketch. If Raphael should come in now he'd make a lovely head of that. Leonardo da Vinci, one of the greatest, would pass months drawing that cheek. You must all do some hard work, or you'll never get anywhere. People say, "That's a horrid daub, — done by one of Hunt's pupils. He never lets them *finish* anything."

Because I let you begin by drawing masses, I don't intend to have you stop there. I want you to go on, and dig and trace, and make outlines, and do all the hard things that anybody does — on the top of a foundation of "values." I don't know that any one ever taught in this way; but it's my way of teaching, and I see no reason for giving it up.

I remember that, when I first took a class, I had no idea how I should conduct it. I went into the large studio full of young ladies whose names even I did not know. I said, "I suppose you all know how to draw?" They thought it necessary to say, "Yes." "Would they draw for me any object that we see every day, a hack, for instance, with horses?" Oh, they couldn't draw that. I mentioned several familiar objects; but they couldn't draw those. I brought them right down to the point, and made them say that they could not draw.

I said, "Drawing is a language; it is a means of expression. If you do not know how to give the impression you have received; you do not know how to draw." I took a familiar object, as simple as a spool of black thread, and pointed out the "values" of the object. There was the highlight on the white spool, first value; next, the middle tint of the spool, second value; the table, the third; the shaded side of the spool, the fourth value; and the black silk, the fifth.

"Now," I continued, "if you give attention to these values I care not how the thing is drawn, — for a spool might be larger or smaller. If you represent these values faithfully you will have the picture."

I do not know if any one ever taught in this method before. I was not taught thus; but I started with the idea of drawing by representing "values," and I have stuck to it ever since.

I also told them to bring in sketches from memory of something they had seen that day. I asked to see what they had brought. Only one responded.

"Will you all turn your work to the wall? In five minutes every one must show me a sketch of something she has seen within the last twenty- four hour, if it is nothing but a ten-penny nail. Four minutes by the watch. Three minutes. Two minutes. Will give you one extra minute. Time's up! Any one here whose name begins with A?" No. "With B?" Miss B. brought her drawing and the others followed, until we had over twenty drawings. After that they were not afraid of each other; all began to draw with a will, and some beautiful drawings from memory were made that winter. I saved them to show what the class had done. It's a pity that they were all burned with my studio.

———————————

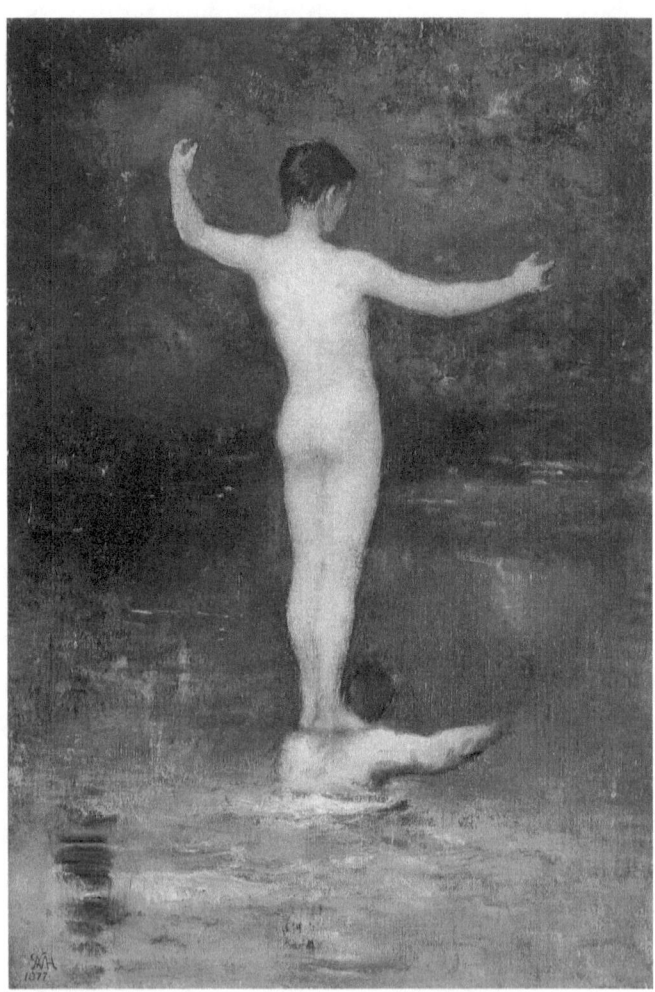

Bathers, 1877, oil, 34x24 inches, Worcester Art Museum.

Epilogue

For oh, this world and the wrong it does!
   They are safe in heaven with their backs to it.
The Michaels and Rafaels, you hum and buzz
   Round the works of, you of the little wit;
Do their eyes contract to the earth's old scope,
   Now that they see God face to face
And have all attained to be poets, I hope?
   'Tis their holiday now, in any case.

Much they reck of your praise and you!
   But the wronged great souls — can they be quit
Of a world where all their work is to do,
   Where you style them, you of the little wit,
Old Master this and Early the other,
   Not dreaming that Old and New are fellows,
That a younger succeeds to an elder brother.
   Da Vincis derive in good time from Dellos.
               — BROWNING

Clara, I hold thee happier specimen, —
It may be, through that artist preference
For work complete, inferiorly proposed.
To incompletion though it aim aright.
Morally, no! Aspire, break bounds! I say,
Endeavour to be good, and better still,
And best! Success is nought, endeavour's all
But intellect adjusts the means to ends,

129

Tries the low thing and leaves it done at Ieast;
No prejudice to high thing, intellect
Would do and will do, only give the means.
Miranda in my picture-gallery,
Presents a Blake; be Clara—Meissonier!
Merely considered so by artist, mind!
For, break through Art, and rise to poetry.
Bring Art to tremble nearer, touch enough
The verge of vastness to inform our soul
What orb makes transit through the dark above,
And there's the triumph! — there the incomplete,
More than completion matches the immense,—
Then Michelangelo against the world!

Well, is the explanation difficult?
What's poetry except a power that makes?
And, speaking to one sense, inspires the rest,
Pressing them all into its service ; so
That who sees painting, seems to hear as well
The speech that's proper for the painted mouth
And who hears music, feels his solitude
Peopled at once — for how count heart-beats plain
Unless a company, with hearts which beat,
Come close to the musician, seen or no?
And who receives true verse at eye or ear.
Takes in (with verse) time, place, and person too,
So, links each sense on to its sister-sense,

Epilogue

Grace-like: and what if but one sense of three
Front you at once? The sidelong pair conceive
Thro' faintest touch of finest finger-tips, —
Hear, see and feel, in faith's simplicity,
Alike, what one was sole recipient of:
Who hears the poem, therefore, sees the play.

      — Browning

Degrade first the Arts if you would
Mankind degrade. — Blake

God's works — paint any one, and count it crime
To let a truth slip. Don't object, "His works
Are here already— nature is complete:
Suppose you reproduce her — (which you can't)
There's no advantage! you must beat her, then."
For, don't you mark, we're made so that we love
First when we see them painted, things we have passed
Perhaps a hundred times nor cared to see;
And so they are better painted — better to us.
Which is the same thing. Art was given for that —
God uses us to help each other so.
Lending our minds out. —

     — Browning

Imagination has nothing to do with memory.

     — Blake

On which I conclude that the early painters,
   To ones of "Greek Art and what more wish you?"
Replied, "Become now self-acquainters,
   And paint man, man, whatever the issue!
Make the hopes shine through the flesh they fray,
   New fears aggrandize the rags and tatters.
So bring the invisible full into play,
   Let the visible go to the dogs — what matters?"

                  — BROWNING

THE refinements not only of execution, but of truth and nature are inaccessible to unpractised eyes. The exquisite gradations in a sky of Claude's are not perceived by such persons, and consequently the harmony cannot be felt. When there is no conscious apprehension there can be no conscious pleasure. Wonder at the first sight of works of art may be the effect of ignorance and novelty; but real admiration and permanent delight in them are the growth of taste and knowledge.

Industry alone can only produce mediocrity; but mediocrity in art is not worth the trouble of industry. Genius, great natural powers, will give industry and ardour in the pursuit of their proper object, but not if you divert them from that object into the trammels of commonplace mechanical labour. By this method you neutralise all distinction of character — make a pedant of the blockhead and a drudge of the man of genius.

                  — HAZLITT

ART is inspiration.— BLAKE

WE are led to believe a lie
When we see with, not through, the eye. — BLAKE

THE eye sees more than the heart knows. — BLAKE

NO ONE who has not devoted his life and soul to the pursuit of art can feel the same exultation in its brightest ornaments and loftiest triumphs that an artist does. Where the treasure is, there the heart is also. — HAZLITT

ENTHUSIASM is the all in all! — BLAKE

RUSKIN ON PUBLIC LECTURES.— Mr. Chapman, convener of the Glasgow Athenæum Lecture Committee, wrote to Mr. Ruskin recently, asking him to lecture at the Athenæum during the winter season. Mr. Ruskin has, in reply, written the following characteristic letter: —

"My Dear Sir,   "Rome, *May* 26, 1874.

"I have your obliging letter, but am compelled, by increase of work, to cease lecturing, except at Oxford — and practically there also — for, indeed, I find the desire of audiences to be audiences only becoming an entirely pestilent character of the age. Everybody wants to hear —nobody to read — nobody to think. To be excited for an hour — and, if possible, amused; to get the knowledge it has cost a man half his life to gather, first sweetened up to make it palatable, and then kneaded into the smallest possible pills — and to swallow it homeopathically and be wise — this is the passionate desire and hope of the multitude of the day. It is not to be done. A living comment quietly given to a class on the book they are earnestly reading— this kind of lecture is eternally necessary and wholesome; your modem fire-working, smooth-downy-curry- and-strawberry-ice-and-milk- punch-altogether lecture is an entirely pestilent and abominable vanity: and the miserable death of I poor Dickens, when he might have been writing books till he was eighty but for the pestiferous demand of the mob, is a very solemn warning to us all, if we would take it. God willing, I will go on writing, and as well as I can. There are three volumes published of my Oxford lectures, in which every sentence is set down as carefully as may be. If people want to learn from me let them read them or my monthly letter, Fors Clavigera. If they don't care for these I don't care to talk to them,

"Truly yours,

"J. RUSKIN"

ANGLUS can never see perfection
But in the journeyman's labour. — BLAKE

THE difference between a bad artist and a good is, that the bad artist *seems* to copy a great deal, the good one *does* copy a great deal.

— Blake

Epilogue

Servile copying is the great merit of copying.

— Blake

So British Public, who may like me yet,
(Marry and amen!) learn one lesson hence
Of many which whatever lives should teach:
This lesson, that our human speech is naught.
Our human testimony false, our fame
And human estimation words and wind.
Why take the artistic way to prove so much?
Because, it is the glory and good of Art,
That Art remains the one way possible
Of speaking truth, to mouths like mine, at least
How look a brother in the face and say,
"Thy sight is wrong— eyes hast thou yet art blind,
Thine ears are stuffed and stopped, despite their length.
And, oh, the foolishness thou countest faith!"
Say this as silverly as tongue can troll —
The anger of the man may be endured,
The shrug, the disappointed eyes of him
Are not so bad to bear — but here's the plague,
That all this trouble comes of telling truth,
Which truth, by when it reaches him, looks false.
Seems to be just the thing it would supplant,
Nor recognizable by whom it left —
While falsehood would have done the work of truth.
But Art, — wherein man nowise speaks to man,

Only to mankind,— Art may tell a truth
Obliquely, as the thing shall breed the thought,
Nor wrong the thought, missing the mediate word.
So may you paint your picture, twice show truth,
Beyond mere imagery on the wall, —
So, note by note, bring music from your mind,
Deeper than ever the Andante dived,—
So write a book shall mean, beyond the facts,
Suffice the eye and save the soul beside.

— BROWNING

ARTISTS ARE supposed to pass their lives in earnest endeavour to express through the medium of paint or pencil, thoughts, feelings, or impressions which they cannot help expressing, and which cannot possibly be expressed by any other means. They make use of material means in order to arrive at this end. They tell their story — the story of a day, an impression of a character, a recollection of a moment, or whatever, more or less clearly or well, as they are more or less capable of doing. They expose their work to the public, not for the sake of praise, but with a feeling and a hope that some human being may see in it the feeling that has passed through their own mind in their poor and necessarily crippled statement. The endeavour is honest and earnest, if almost always with a result weakened by over conscientiousness or endeavour to be understood.

Then the material in which they work is of a nature so

impossible! Imagine! You have never tried it? — this under-taking to render sunlight, life, air, flowers, with the same tarry, unguent substance which you employ to keep wood from water-soak, or which you avoid for fear of having your clothes soiled! For the sign, *"Look out for Paint!"* is hung up with the same universal conscience and has almost as much. power as the ugn "Small-pox here!"

Imagine modelling and rendering youth and beauty in the same substance which you avoid as soiling your boots; or, chiselling and reproducing the smile of an infant from the same ungrateful substance which you use as an ever enduring slab on which to record the fact — to future generations, that under this stone a human being lies buried! Is it not rather a wonder that the painter or sculptor has ever succeeded in doing anything!

Your work is exhibited. Not with the intention of injuring any of the human race. It is a dumb, noiseless, silent story, told, as best it may be, by the author to those whom it may concern.

And it does tell its story. Not to *everybody*. But to *somebody*.

— HUNT